Division Facts Practice Worksheets

Arithmetic Workbook with Answers

Reproducible Timed Math Drills:

Dividing by the Numbers 0-12

Anne Fairbanks

Simple No-Frills Math Sheets

Division Facts Practice Worksheets Arithmetic Workbook with Answers

Reproducible Timed Math Drills: Dividing by the Numbers 0-12

copyright (c) 2011

Anne Fairbanks

Simple No-Frills Math Sheets

Children > Nonfiction > Education > Math > Arithmetic

First edition and first printing in December 2011

ISBN-10:   1468139711   ISBN-13:   978-1468139716

TABLE OF CONTENTS

INTRODUCTION

- This workbook consists of 100 basic division facts worksheets.

- These division drills help to develop fluency in arithmetic.

- All problems involve the numbers 0 thru 12.

- Record the score and time at the top of each worksheet.

- Try to improve your score and time as you continue.

- Check your answers at the back of the workbook.

- Each exercise is numbered for easy reference.

- Teachers may reproduce selected worksheets for their students.

- Includes space for students to write their name at the top.

①
$$8 \div 1$$

②
$$2 \div 1$$

③
$$8 \div 1$$

④
$$4 \div 1$$

⑤
$$6 \div 1$$

⑥
$$8 \div 1$$

⑦
$$7 \div 1$$

⑧
$$1 \div 1$$

⑨
$$7 \div 1$$

⑩
$$1 \div 1$$

⑪
$$4 \div 1$$

⑫
$$6 \div 1$$

⑬
$$1 \div 1$$

⑭
$$9 \div 1$$

⑮
$$10 \div 1$$

⑯
$$7 \div 1$$

⑰
$$8 \div 1$$

⑱
$$3 \div 1$$

⑲
$$0 \div 1$$

⑳
$$0 \div 1$$

㉑
$$10 \div 1$$

㉒
$$0 \div 1$$

㉓
$$9 \div 1$$

㉔
$$4 \div 1$$

㉕
$$9 \div 1$$

㉖
$$8 \div 1$$

㉗
$$1 \div 1$$

㉘
$$1 \div 1$$

㉙
$$8 \div 1$$

㉚
$$6 \div 1$$

㉛
$$0 \div 1$$

㉜
$$6 \div 1$$

㉝
$$8 \div 1$$

㉞
$$10 \div 1$$

㉟
$$1 \div 1$$

①
$$7 \div 1$$

②
$$4 \div 1$$

③
$$0 \div 1$$

④
$$7 \div 1$$

⑤
$$2 \div 1$$

⑥
$$5 \div 1$$

⑦
$$1 \div 1$$

⑧
$$2 \div 1$$

⑨
$$9 \div 1$$

⑩
$$7 \div 1$$

⑪
$$3 \div 1$$

⑫
$$2 \div 1$$

⑬
$$6 \div 1$$

⑭
$$10 \div 1$$

⑮
$$9 \div 1$$

⑯
$$1 \div 1$$

⑰
$$8 \div 1$$

⑱
$$6 \div 1$$

⑲
$$1 \div 1$$

⑳
$$0 \div 1$$

㉑
$$3 \div 1$$

㉒
$$7 \div 1$$

㉓
$$10 \div 1$$

㉔
$$1 \div 1$$

㉕
$$7 \div 1$$

㉖
$$8 \div 1$$

㉗
$$2 \div 1$$

㉘
$$0 \div 1$$

㉙
$$0 \div 1$$

㉚
$$10 \div 1$$

㉛
$$1 \div 1$$

㉜
$$1 \div 1$$

㉝
$$6 \div 1$$

㉞
$$0 \div 1$$

㉟
$$0 \div 1$$

①
16
÷ 2

②
14
÷ 2

③
12
÷ 2

④
16
÷ 2

⑤
10
÷ 2

⑥
20
÷ 2

⑦
8
÷ 2

⑧
0
÷ 2

⑨
2
÷ 2

⑩
2
÷ 2

⑪
16
÷ 2

⑫
8
÷ 2

⑬
4
÷ 2

⑭
14
÷ 2

⑮
16
÷ 2

⑯
6
÷ 2

⑰
8
÷ 2

⑱
20
÷ 2

⑲
12
÷ 2

⑳
12
÷ 2

㉑
2
÷ 2

㉒
8
÷ 2

㉓
14
÷ 2

㉔
4
÷ 2

㉕
16
÷ 2

㉖
0
÷ 2

㉗
16
÷ 2

㉘
4
÷ 2

㉙
18
÷ 2

㉚
2
÷ 2

㉛
0
÷ 2

㉜
18
÷ 2

㉝
0
÷ 2

㉞
18
÷ 2

㉟
8
÷ 2

① 18 ÷ 2

② 12 ÷ 2

③ 18 ÷ 2

④ 2 ÷ 2

⑤ 0 ÷ 2

⑥ 18 ÷ 2

⑦ 0 ÷ 2

⑧ 10 ÷ 2

⑨ 18 ÷ 2

⑩ 2 ÷ 2

⑪ 6 ÷ 2

⑫ 12 ÷ 2

⑬ 16 ÷ 2

⑭ 18 ÷ 2

⑮ 8 ÷ 2

⑯ 8 ÷ 2

⑰ 18 ÷ 2

⑱ 2 ÷ 2

⑲ 16 ÷ 2

⑳ 8 ÷ 2

㉑ 16 ÷ 2

㉒ 6 ÷ 2

㉓ 16 ÷ 2

㉔ 6 ÷ 2

㉕ 6 ÷ 2

㉖ 8 ÷ 2

㉗ 10 ÷ 2

㉘ 0 ÷ 2

㉙ 16 ÷ 2

㉚ 12 ÷ 2

㉛ 4 ÷ 2

㉜ 18 ÷ 2

㉝ 6 ÷ 2

㉞ 16 ÷ 2

㉟ 12 ÷ 2

①
$$15 \div 3$$

②
$$12 \div 3$$

③
$$15 \div 3$$

④
$$24 \div 3$$

⑤
$$9 \div 3$$

⑥
$$12 \div 3$$

⑦
$$3 \div 3$$

⑧
$$15 \div 3$$

⑨
$$18 \div 3$$

⑩
$$12 \div 3$$

⑪
$$18 \div 3$$

⑫
$$30 \div 3$$

⑬
$$3 \div 3$$

⑭
$$24 \div 3$$

⑮
$$15 \div 3$$

⑯
$$30 \div 3$$

⑰
$$3 \div 3$$

⑱
$$21 \div 3$$

⑲
$$3 \div 3$$

⑳
$$18 \div 3$$

㉑
$$15 \div 3$$

㉒
$$18 \div 3$$

㉓
$$27 \div 3$$

㉔
$$18 \div 3$$

㉕
$$9 \div 3$$

㉖
$$27 \div 3$$

㉗
$$24 \div 3$$

㉘
$$18 \div 3$$

㉙
$$24 \div 3$$

㉚
$$15 \div 3$$

㉛
$$15 \div 3$$

㉜
$$12 \div 3$$

㉝
$$3 \div 3$$

㉞
$$30 \div 3$$

㉟
$$6 \div 3$$

①
  30
÷ 3
————

②
  18
÷ 3
————

③
  18
÷ 3
————

④
  21
÷ 3
————

⑤
  15
÷ 3
————

⑥
  0
÷ 3
————

⑦
  21
÷ 3
————

⑧
  24
÷ 3
————

⑨
  21
÷ 3
————

⑩
  18
÷ 3
————

⑪
  12
÷ 3
————

⑫
  6
÷ 3
————

⑬
  30
÷ 3
————

⑭
  6
÷ 3
————

⑮
  6
÷ 3
————

⑯
  27
÷ 3
————

⑰
  30
÷ 3
————

⑱
  30
÷ 3
————

⑲
  18
÷ 3
————

⑳
  15
÷ 3
————

㉑
  6
÷ 3
————

㉒
  21
÷ 3
————

㉓
  0
÷ 3
————

㉔
  15
÷ 3
————

㉕
  24
÷ 3
————

㉖
  3
÷ 3
————

㉗
  15
÷ 3
————

㉘
  12
÷ 3
————

㉙
  24
÷ 3
————

㉚
  30
÷ 3
————

㉛
  18
÷ 3
————

㉜
  27
÷ 3
————

㉝
  9
÷ 3
————

㉞
  12
÷ 3
————

㉟
  0
÷ 3
————

① 12 ÷ 4

② 28 ÷ 4

③ 0 ÷ 4

④ 40 ÷ 4

⑤ 12 ÷ 4

⑥ 36 ÷ 4

⑦ 20 ÷ 4

⑧ 24 ÷ 4

⑨ 8 ÷ 4

⑩ 8 ÷ 4

⑪ 28 ÷ 4

⑫ 8 ÷ 4

⑬ 0 ÷ 4

⑭ 4 ÷ 4

⑮ 36 ÷ 4

⑯ 16 ÷ 4

⑰ 24 ÷ 4

⑱ 16 ÷ 4

⑲ 36 ÷ 4

⑳ 40 ÷ 4

㉑ 12 ÷ 4

㉒ 20 ÷ 4

㉓ 12 ÷ 4

㉔ 36 ÷ 4

㉕ 40 ÷ 4

㉖ 12 ÷ 4

㉗ 36 ÷ 4

㉘ 24 ÷ 4

㉙ 8 ÷ 4

㉚ 32 ÷ 4

㉛ 20 ÷ 4

㉜ 28 ÷ 4

㉝ 8 ÷ 4

㉞ 40 ÷ 4

㉟ 8 ÷ 4

①
40
÷ 4

②
28
÷ 4

③
8
÷ 4

④
36
÷ 4

⑤
12
÷ 4

⑥
16
÷ 4

⑦
16
÷ 4

⑧
12
÷ 4

⑨
36
÷ 4

⑩
8
÷ 4

⑪
12
÷ 4

⑫
36
÷ 4

⑬
28
÷ 4

⑭
8
÷ 4

⑮
8
÷ 4

⑯
28
÷ 4

⑰
40
÷ 4

⑱
40
÷ 4

⑲
0
÷ 4

⑳
8
÷ 4

㉑
40
÷ 4

㉒
40
÷ 4

㉓
36
÷ 4

㉔
28
÷ 4

㉕
0
÷ 4

㉖
20
÷ 4

㉗
24
÷ 4

㉘
20
÷ 4

㉙
28
÷ 4

㉚
36
÷ 4

㉛
40
÷ 4

㉜
36
÷ 4

㉝
40
÷ 4

㉞
20
÷ 4

㉟
8
÷ 4

① 15 ÷ 5

② 25 ÷ 5

③ 30 ÷ 5

④ 40 ÷ 5

⑤ 15 ÷ 5

⑥ 25 ÷ 5

⑦ 45 ÷ 5

⑧ 35 ÷ 5

⑨ 50 ÷ 5

⑩ 20 ÷ 5

⑪ 5 ÷ 5

⑫ 40 ÷ 5

⑬ 10 ÷ 5

⑭ 50 ÷ 5

⑮ 45 ÷ 5

⑯ 15 ÷ 5

⑰ 30 ÷ 5

⑱ 0 ÷ 5

⑲ 20 ÷ 5

⑳ 0 ÷ 5

㉑ 35 ÷ 5

㉒ 45 ÷ 5

㉓ 25 ÷ 5

㉔ 30 ÷ 5

㉕ 10 ÷ 5

㉖ 45 ÷ 5

㉗ 15 ÷ 5

㉘ 50 ÷ 5

㉙ 15 ÷ 5

㉚ 30 ÷ 5

㉛ 0 ÷ 5

㉜ 30 ÷ 5

㉝ 35 ÷ 5

㉞ 30 ÷ 5

㉟ 45 ÷ 5

① 25 ÷ 5

② 40 ÷ 5

③ 0 ÷ 5

④ 0 ÷ 5

⑤ 30 ÷ 5

⑥ 10 ÷ 5

⑦ 50 ÷ 5

⑧ 5 ÷ 5

⑨ 5 ÷ 5

⑩ 20 ÷ 5

⑪ 50 ÷ 5

⑫ 50 ÷ 5

⑬ 40 ÷ 5

⑭ 50 ÷ 5

⑮ 35 ÷ 5

⑯ 40 ÷ 5

⑰ 10 ÷ 5

⑱ 0 ÷ 5

⑲ 15 ÷ 5

⑳ 5 ÷ 5

㉑ 30 ÷ 5

㉒ 35 ÷ 5

㉓ 30 ÷ 5

㉔ 45 ÷ 5

㉕ 50 ÷ 5

㉖ 5 ÷ 5

㉗ 15 ÷ 5

㉘ 30 ÷ 5

㉙ 10 ÷ 5

㉚ 50 ÷ 5

㉛ 35 ÷ 5

㉜ 10 ÷ 5

㉝ 10 ÷ 5

㉞ 50 ÷ 5

㉟ 40 ÷ 5

①
54
÷ 6

②
48
÷ 6

③
12
÷ 6

④
0
÷ 6

⑤
6
÷ 6

⑥
6
÷ 6

⑦
0
÷ 6

⑧
12
÷ 6

⑨
6
÷ 6

⑩
60
÷ 6

⑪
60
÷ 6

⑫
30
÷ 6

⑬
36
÷ 6

⑭
36
÷ 6

⑮
24
÷ 6

⑯
0
÷ 6

⑰
0
÷ 6

⑱
18
÷ 6

⑲
60
÷ 6

⑳
24
÷ 6

㉑
18
÷ 6

㉒
36
÷ 6

㉓
30
÷ 6

㉔
12
÷ 6

㉕
42
÷ 6

㉖
18
÷ 6

㉗
18
÷ 6

㉘
12
÷ 6

㉙
18
÷ 6

㉚
54
÷ 6

㉛
24
÷ 6

㉜
30
÷ 6

㉝
0
÷ 6

㉞
48
÷ 6

㉟
6
÷ 6

①
  12
÷ 6

②
  54
÷ 6

③
  42
÷ 6

④
  54
÷ 6

⑤
  18
÷ 6

⑥
  0
÷ 6

⑦
  48
÷ 6

⑧
  30
÷ 6

⑨
  0
÷ 6

⑩
  42
÷ 6

⑪
  42
÷ 6

⑫
  12
÷ 6

⑬
  6
÷ 6

⑭
  18
÷ 6

⑮
  42
÷ 6

⑯
  24
÷ 6

⑰
  42
÷ 6

⑱
  36
÷ 6

⑲
  42
÷ 6

⑳
  48
÷ 6

㉑
  24
÷ 6

㉒
  0
÷ 6

㉓
  24
÷ 6

㉔
  42
÷ 6

㉕
  6
÷ 6

㉖
  24
÷ 6

㉗
  12
÷ 6

㉘
  54
÷ 6

㉙
  48
÷ 6

㉚
  30
÷ 6

㉛
  42
÷ 6

㉜
  30
÷ 6

㉝
  24
÷ 6

㉞
  18
÷ 6

㉟
  54
÷ 6

①
70
÷ 7

②
35
÷ 7

③
28
÷ 7

④
7
÷ 7

⑤
21
÷ 7

⑥
56
÷ 7

⑦
35
÷ 7

⑧
0
÷ 7

⑨
28
÷ 7

⑩
28
÷ 7

⑪
14
÷ 7

⑫
42
÷ 7

⑬
35
÷ 7

⑭
21
÷ 7

⑮
21
÷ 7

⑯
49
÷ 7

⑰
42
÷ 7

⑱
0
÷ 7

⑲
70
÷ 7

⑳
14
÷ 7

㉑
28
÷ 7

㉒
56
÷ 7

㉓
21
÷ 7

㉔
49
÷ 7

㉕
0
÷ 7

㉖
21
÷ 7

㉗
49
÷ 7

㉘
56
÷ 7

㉙
14
÷ 7

㉚
21
÷ 7

㉛
7
÷ 7

㉜
0
÷ 7

㉝
42
÷ 7

㉞
28
÷ 7

㉟
35
÷ 7

① 49 ÷ 7

② 7 ÷ 7

③ 7 ÷ 7

④ 28 ÷ 7

⑤ 49 ÷ 7

⑥ 56 ÷ 7

⑦ 42 ÷ 7

⑧ 63 ÷ 7

⑨ 7 ÷ 7

⑩ 70 ÷ 7

⑪ 7 ÷ 7

⑫ 63 ÷ 7

⑬ 35 ÷ 7

⑭ 63 ÷ 7

⑮ 14 ÷ 7

⑯ 63 ÷ 7

⑰ 0 ÷ 7

⑱ 70 ÷ 7

⑲ 35 ÷ 7

⑳ 14 ÷ 7

㉑ 7 ÷ 7

㉒ 28 ÷ 7

㉓ 70 ÷ 7

㉔ 42 ÷ 7

㉕ 56 ÷ 7

㉖ 70 ÷ 7

㉗ 42 ÷ 7

㉘ 7 ÷ 7

㉙ 0 ÷ 7

㉚ 21 ÷ 7

㉛ 63 ÷ 7

㉜ 21 ÷ 7

㉝ 42 ÷ 7

㉞ 42 ÷ 7

㉟ 0 ÷ 7

①
16
÷ 8

②
24
÷ 8

③
64
÷ 8

④
48
÷ 8

⑤
80
÷ 8

⑥
56
÷ 8

⑦
16
÷ 8

⑧
48
÷ 8

⑨
24
÷ 8

⑩
48
÷ 8

⑪
40
÷ 8

⑫
0
÷ 8

⑬
16
÷ 8

⑭
64
÷ 8

⑮
40
÷ 8

⑯
24
÷ 8

⑰
32
÷ 8

⑱
24
÷ 8

⑲
80
÷ 8

⑳
32
÷ 8

㉑
8
÷ 8

㉒
80
÷ 8

㉓
32
÷ 8

㉔
0
÷ 8

㉕
16
÷ 8

㉖
56
÷ 8

㉗
56
÷ 8

㉘
64
÷ 8

㉙
40
÷ 8

㉚
64
÷ 8

㉛
80
÷ 8

㉜
40
÷ 8

㉝
64
÷ 8

㉞
56
÷ 8

㉟
32
÷ 8

①
80
÷ 8

②
56
÷ 8

③
24
÷ 8

④
80
÷ 8

⑤
72
÷ 8

⑥
8
÷ 8

⑦
56
÷ 8

⑧
64
÷ 8

⑨
72
÷ 8

⑩
56
÷ 8

⑪
16
÷ 8

⑫
56
÷ 8

⑬
80
÷ 8

⑭
32
÷ 8

⑮
72
÷ 8

⑯
16
÷ 8

⑰
8
÷ 8

⑱
40
÷ 8

⑲
80
÷ 8

⑳
48
÷ 8

㉑
64
÷ 8

㉒
80
÷ 8

㉓
56
÷ 8

㉔
72
÷ 8

㉕
48
÷ 8

㉖
24
÷ 8

㉗
56
÷ 8

㉘
80
÷ 8

㉙
8
÷ 8

㉚
40
÷ 8

㉛
48
÷ 8

㉜
32
÷ 8

㉝
32
÷ 8

㉞
48
÷ 8

㉟
80
÷ 8

Score		Time		Worksheet 17	Name	

①
81
÷ 9

②
18
÷ 9

③
9
÷ 9

④
36
÷ 9

⑤
90
÷ 9

⑥
54
÷ 9

⑦
90
÷ 9

⑧
54
÷ 9

⑨
72
÷ 9

⑩
36
÷ 9

⑪
45
÷ 9

⑫
18
÷ 9

⑬
36
÷ 9

⑭
18
÷ 9

⑮
36
÷ 9

⑯
36
÷ 9

⑰
0
÷ 9

⑱
0
÷ 9

⑲
81
÷ 9

⑳
90
÷ 9

㉑
72
÷ 9

㉒
63
÷ 9

㉓
9
÷ 9

㉔
9
÷ 9

㉕
81
÷ 9

㉖
90
÷ 9

㉗
18
÷ 9

㉘
27
÷ 9

㉙
9
÷ 9

㉚
0
÷ 9

㉛
72
÷ 9

㉜
18
÷ 9

㉝
54
÷ 9

㉞
27
÷ 9

㉟
36
÷ 9

①
$$\begin{array}{r} 36 \\ \div\ 9 \\ \hline \end{array}$$

②
$$\begin{array}{r} 36 \\ \div\ 9 \\ \hline \end{array}$$

③
$$\begin{array}{r} 36 \\ \div\ 9 \\ \hline \end{array}$$

④
$$\begin{array}{r} 27 \\ \div\ 9 \\ \hline \end{array}$$

⑤
$$\begin{array}{r} 36 \\ \div\ 9 \\ \hline \end{array}$$

⑥
$$\begin{array}{r} 81 \\ \div\ 9 \\ \hline \end{array}$$

⑦
$$\begin{array}{r} 27 \\ \div\ 9 \\ \hline \end{array}$$

⑧
$$\begin{array}{r} 81 \\ \div\ 9 \\ \hline \end{array}$$

⑨
$$\begin{array}{r} 27 \\ \div\ 9 \\ \hline \end{array}$$

⑩
$$\begin{array}{r} 9 \\ \div\ 9 \\ \hline \end{array}$$

⑪
$$\begin{array}{r} 54 \\ \div\ 9 \\ \hline \end{array}$$

⑫
$$\begin{array}{r} 18 \\ \div\ 9 \\ \hline \end{array}$$

⑬
$$\begin{array}{r} 45 \\ \div\ 9 \\ \hline \end{array}$$

⑭
$$\begin{array}{r} 45 \\ \div\ 9 \\ \hline \end{array}$$

⑮
$$\begin{array}{r} 0 \\ \div\ 9 \\ \hline \end{array}$$

⑯
$$\begin{array}{r} 27 \\ \div\ 9 \\ \hline \end{array}$$

⑰
$$\begin{array}{r} 0 \\ \div\ 9 \\ \hline \end{array}$$

⑱
$$\begin{array}{r} 36 \\ \div\ 9 \\ \hline \end{array}$$

⑲
$$\begin{array}{r} 45 \\ \div\ 9 \\ \hline \end{array}$$

⑳
$$\begin{array}{r} 18 \\ \div\ 9 \\ \hline \end{array}$$

㉑
$$\begin{array}{r} 54 \\ \div\ 9 \\ \hline \end{array}$$

㉒
$$\begin{array}{r} 18 \\ \div\ 9 \\ \hline \end{array}$$

㉓
$$\begin{array}{r} 63 \\ \div\ 9 \\ \hline \end{array}$$

㉔
$$\begin{array}{r} 90 \\ \div\ 9 \\ \hline \end{array}$$

㉕
$$\begin{array}{r} 54 \\ \div\ 9 \\ \hline \end{array}$$

㉖
$$\begin{array}{r} 27 \\ \div\ 9 \\ \hline \end{array}$$

㉗
$$\begin{array}{r} 54 \\ \div\ 9 \\ \hline \end{array}$$

㉘
$$\begin{array}{r} 45 \\ \div\ 9 \\ \hline \end{array}$$

㉙
$$\begin{array}{r} 18 \\ \div\ 9 \\ \hline \end{array}$$

㉚
$$\begin{array}{r} 63 \\ \div\ 9 \\ \hline \end{array}$$

㉛
$$\begin{array}{r} 18 \\ \div\ 9 \\ \hline \end{array}$$

㉜
$$\begin{array}{r} 36 \\ \div\ 9 \\ \hline \end{array}$$

㉝
$$\begin{array}{r} 90 \\ \div\ 9 \\ \hline \end{array}$$

㉞
$$\begin{array}{r} 54 \\ \div\ 9 \\ \hline \end{array}$$

㉟
$$\begin{array}{r} 27 \\ \div\ 9 \\ \hline \end{array}$$

①
60
÷ 10

②
50
÷ 10

③
50
÷ 10

④
70
÷ 10

⑤
60
÷ 10

⑥
70
÷ 10

⑦
30
÷ 10

⑧
0
÷ 10

⑨
0
÷ 10

⑩
0
÷ 10

⑪
0
÷ 10

⑫
20
÷ 10

⑬
10
÷ 10

⑭
90
÷ 10

⑮
100
÷ 10

⑯
90
÷ 10

⑰
60
÷ 10

⑱
100
÷ 10

⑲
100
÷ 10

⑳
0
÷ 10

㉑
50
÷ 10

㉒
30
÷ 10

㉓
40
÷ 10

㉔
30
÷ 10

㉕
40
÷ 10

㉖
0
÷ 10

㉗
80
÷ 10

㉘
20
÷ 10

㉙
20
÷ 10

㉚
20
÷ 10

㉛
0
÷ 10

㉜
0
÷ 10

㉝
10
÷ 10

㉞
80
÷ 10

㉟
10
÷ 10

①
$$30 \div 10$$

②
$$60 \div 10$$

③
$$50 \div 10$$

④
$$10 \div 10$$

⑤
$$70 \div 10$$

⑥
$$10 \div 10$$

⑦
$$90 \div 10$$

⑧
$$80 \div 10$$

⑨
$$50 \div 10$$

⑩
$$70 \div 10$$

⑪
$$30 \div 10$$

⑫
$$40 \div 10$$

⑬
$$10 \div 10$$

⑭
$$0 \div 10$$

⑮
$$20 \div 10$$

⑯
$$100 \div 10$$

⑰
$$80 \div 10$$

⑱
$$40 \div 10$$

⑲
$$0 \div 10$$

⑳
$$10 \div 10$$

㉑
$$100 \div 10$$

㉒
$$20 \div 10$$

㉓
$$80 \div 10$$

㉔
$$20 \div 10$$

㉕
$$10 \div 10$$

㉖
$$100 \div 10$$

㉗
$$30 \div 10$$

㉘
$$60 \div 10$$

㉙
$$30 \div 10$$

㉚
$$100 \div 10$$

㉛
$$50 \div 10$$

㉜
$$10 \div 10$$

㉝
$$50 \div 10$$

㉞
$$100 \div 10$$

㉟
$$50 \div 10$$

① 3 ÷ 3

② 63 ÷ 9

③ 16 ÷ 4

④ 30 ÷ 5

⑤ 42 ÷ 6

⑥ 24 ÷ 4

⑦ 0 ÷ 6

⑧ 30 ÷ 6

⑨ 100 ÷ 10

⑩ 9 ÷ 1

⑪ 70 ÷ 10

⑫ 40 ÷ 5

⑬ 10 ÷ 2

⑭ 32 ÷ 4

⑮ 40 ÷ 4

⑯ 20 ÷ 4

⑰ 32 ÷ 8

⑱ 0 ÷ 2

⑲ 10 ÷ 1

⑳ 40 ÷ 4

㉑ 60 ÷ 10

㉒ 63 ÷ 9

㉓ 24 ÷ 6

㉔ 10 ÷ 5

㉕ 40 ÷ 8

㉖ 24 ÷ 8

㉗ 54 ÷ 6

㉘ 54 ÷ 9

㉙ 40 ÷ 8

㉚ 0 ÷ 8

㉛ 12 ÷ 4

㉜ 4 ÷ 2

㉝ 0 ÷ 1

㉞ 40 ÷ 5

㉟ 27 ÷ 9

①
$$1 \div 1$$

②
$$48 \div 6$$

③
$$48 \div 8$$

④
$$25 \div 5$$

⑤
$$14 \div 7$$

⑥
$$24 \div 4$$

⑦
$$32 \div 4$$

⑧
$$90 \div 9$$

⑨
$$10 \div 2$$

⑩
$$24 \div 8$$

⑪
$$12 \div 2$$

⑫
$$10 \div 2$$

⑬
$$8 \div 1$$

⑭
$$80 \div 8$$

⑮
$$30 \div 5$$

⑯
$$10 \div 10$$

⑰
$$56 \div 8$$

⑱
$$7 \div 7$$

⑲
$$72 \div 9$$

⑳
$$45 \div 5$$

㉑
$$20 \div 5$$

㉒
$$56 \div 8$$

㉓
$$20 \div 10$$

㉔
$$9 \div 3$$

㉕
$$15 \div 5$$

㉖
$$18 \div 3$$

㉗
$$30 \div 6$$

㉘
$$16 \div 2$$

㉙
$$28 \div 4$$

㉚
$$20 \div 10$$

㉛
$$30 \div 10$$

㉜
$$12 \div 4$$

㉝
$$32 \div 4$$

㉞
$$4 \div 1$$

㉟
$$70 \div 10$$

①
25
÷ 5

②
0
÷ 8

③
6
÷ 2

④
45
÷ 9

⑤
80
÷ 8

⑥
0
÷ 10

⑦
54
÷ 9

⑧
35
÷ 5

⑨
15
÷ 5

⑩
9
÷ 3

⑪
56
÷ 8

⑫
10
÷ 10

⑬
90
÷ 10

⑭
16
÷ 2

⑮
15
÷ 5

⑯
0
÷ 6

⑰
0
÷ 10

⑱
18
÷ 6

⑲
14
÷ 2

⑳
30
÷ 6

㉑
20
÷ 4

㉒
10
÷ 5

㉓
18
÷ 3

㉔
70
÷ 10

㉕
7
÷ 1

㉖
45
÷ 5

㉗
42
÷ 6

㉘
24
÷ 4

㉙
54
÷ 9

㉚
0
÷ 2

㉛
56
÷ 7

㉜
6
÷ 6

㉝
56
÷ 8

㉞
18
÷ 6

㉟
3
÷ 3

①
80
÷ 10

②
72
÷ 8

③
9
÷ 9

④
0
÷ 6

⑤
35
÷ 5

⑥
0
÷ 10

⑦
0
÷ 5

⑧
36
÷ 6

⑨
15
÷ 3

⑩
35
÷ 5

⑪
21
÷ 7

⑫
48
÷ 6

⑬
4
÷ 1

⑭
54
÷ 9

⑮
12
÷ 6

⑯
90
÷ 10

⑰
54
÷ 9

⑱
36
÷ 4

⑲
6
÷ 3

⑳
2
÷ 2

㉑
56
÷ 7

㉒
63
÷ 7

㉓
18
÷ 3

㉔
12
÷ 6

㉕
18
÷ 9

㉖
0
÷ 10

㉗
45
÷ 9

㉘
0
÷ 6

㉙
20
÷ 5

㉚
40
÷ 10

㉛
4
÷ 1

㉜
36
÷ 6

㉝
10
÷ 5

㉞
8
÷ 2

㉟
3
÷ 3

① 48 ÷ 6

② 7 ÷ 7

③ 8 ÷ 4

④ 8 ÷ 2

⑤ 27 ÷ 3

⑥ 50 ÷ 5

⑦ 32 ÷ 4

⑧ 100 ÷ 10

⑨ 32 ÷ 4

⑩ 40 ÷ 5

⑪ 36 ÷ 9

⑫ 27 ÷ 9

⑬ 21 ÷ 7

⑭ 20 ÷ 5

⑮ 0 ÷ 2

⑯ 6 ÷ 1

⑰ 12 ÷ 6

⑱ 12 ÷ 4

⑲ 20 ÷ 4

⑳ 36 ÷ 4

㉑ 48 ÷ 6

㉒ 42 ÷ 7

㉓ 60 ÷ 10

㉔ 100 ÷ 10

㉕ 48 ÷ 6

㉖ 72 ÷ 9

㉗ 24 ÷ 3

㉘ 42 ÷ 7

㉙ 40 ÷ 4

㉚ 40 ÷ 10

㉛ 42 ÷ 7

㉜ 14 ÷ 2

㉝ 24 ÷ 4

㉞ 8 ÷ 4

㉟ 8 ÷ 4

①
$$60 \div 10$$

②
$$40 \div 5$$

③
$$60 \div 6$$

④
$$54 \div 6$$

⑤
$$16 \div 4$$

⑥
$$80 \div 8$$

⑦
$$63 \div 7$$

⑧
$$0 \div 8$$

⑨
$$24 \div 8$$

⑩
$$72 \div 9$$

⑪
$$16 \div 8$$

⑫
$$6 \div 3$$

⑬
$$60 \div 6$$

⑭
$$0 \div 10$$

⑮
$$8 \div 2$$

⑯
$$28 \div 4$$

⑰
$$50 \div 10$$

⑱
$$50 \div 5$$

⑲
$$60 \div 10$$

⑳
$$6 \div 3$$

㉑
$$14 \div 7$$

㉒
$$30 \div 3$$

㉓
$$12 \div 4$$

㉔
$$5 \div 1$$

㉕
$$20 \div 2$$

㉖
$$7 \div 1$$

㉗
$$0 \div 4$$

㉘
$$7 \div 1$$

㉙
$$81 \div 9$$

㉚
$$3 \div 1$$

㉛
$$48 \div 6$$

㉜
$$12 \div 4$$

㉝
$$1 \div 1$$

㉞
$$10 \div 1$$

㉟
$$32 \div 8$$

①   25 ÷ 5

②   4 ÷ 2

③   54 ÷ 9

④   32 ÷ 8

⑤   36 ÷ 6

⑥   3 ÷ 1

⑦   8 ÷ 4

⑧   3 ÷ 1

⑨   24 ÷ 4

⑩   3 ÷ 1

⑪   0 ÷ 9

⑫   0 ÷ 3

⑬   36 ÷ 6

⑭   20 ÷ 5

⑮   4 ÷ 2

⑯   16 ÷ 4

⑰   25 ÷ 5

⑱   40 ÷ 4

⑲   8 ÷ 1

⑳   0 ÷ 1

㉑   24 ÷ 6

㉒   16 ÷ 2

㉓   30 ÷ 6

㉔   28 ÷ 7

㉕   100 ÷ 10

㉖   45 ÷ 5

㉗   6 ÷ 2

㉘   15 ÷ 5

㉙   7 ÷ 1

㉚   36 ÷ 6

㉛   0 ÷ 10

㉜   24 ÷ 4

㉝   0 ÷ 1

㉞   3 ÷ 3

㉟   3 ÷ 1

①
$$10 \div 10$$

②
$$100 \div 10$$

③
$$54 \div 6$$

④
$$81 \div 9$$

⑤
$$6 \div 6$$

⑥
$$27 \div 9$$

⑦
$$20 \div 2$$

⑧
$$36 \div 9$$

⑨
$$24 \div 4$$

⑩
$$8 \div 1$$

⑪
$$18 \div 2$$

⑫
$$3 \div 1$$

⑬
$$14 \div 2$$

⑭
$$7 \div 1$$

⑮
$$100 \div 10$$

⑯
$$35 \div 5$$

⑰
$$14 \div 2$$

⑱
$$6 \div 1$$

⑲
$$20 \div 5$$

⑳
$$40 \div 5$$

㉑
$$4 \div 2$$

㉒
$$35 \div 5$$

㉓
$$30 \div 3$$

㉔
$$27 \div 9$$

㉕
$$81 \div 9$$

㉖
$$10 \div 10$$

㉗
$$15 \div 5$$

㉘
$$27 \div 9$$

㉙
$$36 \div 9$$

㉚
$$30 \div 5$$

㉛
$$0 \div 5$$

㉜
$$70 \div 7$$

㉝
$$6 \div 3$$

㉞
$$21 \div 3$$

㉟
$$36 \div 6$$

① 81 ÷ 9

② 6 ÷ 3

③ 72 ÷ 9

④ 40 ÷ 8

⑤ 5 ÷ 1

⑥ 32 ÷ 8

⑦ 21 ÷ 7

⑧ 9 ÷ 3

⑨ 5 ÷ 1

⑩ 27 ÷ 3

⑪ 40 ÷ 10

⑫ 60 ÷ 6

⑬ 54 ÷ 6

⑭ 42 ÷ 7

⑮ 6 ÷ 1

⑯ 16 ÷ 8

⑰ 8 ÷ 1

⑱ 5 ÷ 1

⑲ 32 ÷ 4

⑳ 3 ÷ 3

㉑ 20 ÷ 2

㉒ 27 ÷ 9

㉓ 50 ÷ 10

㉔ 9 ÷ 1

㉕ 25 ÷ 5

㉖ 16 ÷ 2

㉗ 63 ÷ 9

㉘ 90 ÷ 10

㉙ 0 ÷ 5

㉚ 40 ÷ 4

㉛ 36 ÷ 9

㉜ 49 ÷ 7

㉝ 21 ÷ 3

㉞ 36 ÷ 9

㉟ 3 ÷ 1

① 49 ÷ 7

② 40 ÷ 5

③ 24 ÷ 6

④ 21 ÷ 7

⑤ 0 ÷ 4

⑥ 10 ÷ 2

⑦ 90 ÷ 10

⑧ 18 ÷ 9

⑨ 10 ÷ 5

⑩ 48 ÷ 6

⑪ 3 ÷ 3

⑫ 12 ÷ 4

⑬ 40 ÷ 5

⑭ 15 ÷ 5

⑮ 20 ÷ 5

⑯ 35 ÷ 7

⑰ 48 ÷ 8

⑱ 45 ÷ 9

⑲ 0 ÷ 7

⑳ 6 ÷ 3

㉑ 0 ÷ 7

㉒ 14 ÷ 7

㉓ 49 ÷ 7

㉔ 16 ÷ 4

㉕ 8 ÷ 4

㉖ 63 ÷ 7

㉗ 100 ÷ 10

㉘ 30 ÷ 3

㉙ 60 ÷ 6

㉚ 14 ÷ 2

㉛ 2 ÷ 1

㉜ 12 ÷ 2

㉝ 12 ÷ 2

㉞ 18 ÷ 2

㉟ 12 ÷ 3

① 56 ÷ 7

② 40 ÷ 10

③ 8 ÷ 2

④ 40 ÷ 8

⑤ 30 ÷ 6

⑥ 60 ÷ 10

⑦ 45 ÷ 9

⑧ 63 ÷ 9

⑨ 64 ÷ 8

⑩ 30 ÷ 10

⑪ 12 ÷ 3

⑫ 24 ÷ 3

⑬ 42 ÷ 7

⑭ 21 ÷ 3

⑮ 16 ÷ 8

⑯ 45 ÷ 9

⑰ 50 ÷ 5

⑱ 21 ÷ 3

⑲ 16 ÷ 2

⑳ 30 ÷ 3

㉑ 30 ÷ 5

㉒ 35 ÷ 7

㉓ 48 ÷ 6

㉔ 48 ÷ 8

㉕ 32 ÷ 4

㉖ 24 ÷ 4

㉗ 60 ÷ 6

㉘ 90 ÷ 10

㉙ 30 ÷ 5

㉚ 24 ÷ 4

㉛ 16 ÷ 4

㉜ 24 ÷ 6

㉝ 8 ÷ 2

㉞ 20 ÷ 2

㉟ 64 ÷ 8

① 48 ÷ 8

② 6 ÷ 3

③ 36 ÷ 9

④ 21 ÷ 3

⑤ 40 ÷ 8

⑥ 81 ÷ 9

⑦ 18 ÷ 6

⑧ 56 ÷ 7

⑨ 27 ÷ 3

⑩ 16 ÷ 4

⑪ 70 ÷ 10

⑫ 12 ÷ 6

⑬ 54 ÷ 6

⑭ 6 ÷ 2

⑮ 32 ÷ 4

⑯ 27 ÷ 9

⑰ 10 ÷ 2

⑱ 32 ÷ 4

⑲ 6 ÷ 3

⑳ 54 ÷ 9

㉑ 21 ÷ 7

㉒ 28 ÷ 4

㉓ 8 ÷ 2

㉔ 35 ÷ 7

㉕ 30 ÷ 10

㉖ 35 ÷ 5

㉗ 63 ÷ 9

㉘ 49 ÷ 7

㉙ 6 ÷ 2

㉚ 80 ÷ 10

㉛ 45 ÷ 9

㉜ 42 ÷ 7

㉝ 18 ÷ 9

㉞ 14 ÷ 2

㉟ 70 ÷ 7

① 15 ÷ 5

② 90 ÷ 9

③ 100 ÷ 10

④ 25 ÷ 5

⑤ 72 ÷ 9

⑥ 20 ÷ 5

⑦ 20 ÷ 2

⑧ 42 ÷ 7

⑨ 30 ÷ 10

⑩ 18 ÷ 2

⑪ 81 ÷ 9

⑫ 40 ÷ 5

⑬ 12 ÷ 6

⑭ 36 ÷ 9

⑮ 18 ÷ 2

⑯ 30 ÷ 6

⑰ 54 ÷ 6

⑱ 25 ÷ 5

⑲ 12 ÷ 2

⑳ 8 ÷ 2

㉑ 45 ÷ 9

㉒ 20 ÷ 2

㉓ 36 ÷ 6

㉔ 18 ÷ 3

㉕ 21 ÷ 3

㉖ 15 ÷ 3

㉗ 36 ÷ 4

㉘ 15 ÷ 5

㉙ 20 ÷ 4

㉚ 12 ÷ 3

㉛ 70 ÷ 7

㉜ 4 ÷ 2

㉝ 36 ÷ 9

㉞ 56 ÷ 7

㉟ 32 ÷ 8

① 48 ÷ 6

② 60 ÷ 10

③ 30 ÷ 6

④ 9 ÷ 3

⑤ 15 ÷ 5

⑥ 10 ÷ 2

⑦ 24 ÷ 4

⑧ 20 ÷ 2

⑨ 24 ÷ 8

⑩ 64 ÷ 8

⑪ 8 ÷ 4

⑫ 32 ÷ 8

⑬ 12 ÷ 3

⑭ 81 ÷ 9

⑮ 60 ÷ 6

⑯ 16 ÷ 4

⑰ 20 ÷ 10

⑱ 90 ÷ 9

⑲ 45 ÷ 9

⑳ 24 ÷ 3

㉑ 42 ÷ 6

㉒ 56 ÷ 7

㉓ 25 ÷ 5

㉔ 12 ÷ 6

㉕ 8 ÷ 2

㉖ 27 ÷ 3

㉗ 8 ÷ 4

㉘ 16 ÷ 2

㉙ 30 ÷ 6

㉚ 36 ÷ 4

㉛ 30 ÷ 10

㉜ 40 ÷ 5

㉝ 42 ÷ 7

㉞ 80 ÷ 10

㉟ 8 ÷ 2

① 70 ÷ 7

② 8 ÷ 4

③ 24 ÷ 3

④ 54 ÷ 6

⑤ 50 ÷ 5

⑥ 42 ÷ 7

⑦ 12 ÷ 4

⑧ 64 ÷ 8

⑨ 30 ÷ 5

⑩ 15 ÷ 5

⑪ 30 ÷ 5

⑫ 25 ÷ 5

⑬ 15 ÷ 5

⑭ 14 ÷ 2

⑮ 21 ÷ 3

⑯ 35 ÷ 7

⑰ 60 ÷ 10

⑱ 72 ÷ 9

⑲ 18 ÷ 2

⑳ 14 ÷ 7

㉑ 8 ÷ 4

㉒ 28 ÷ 7

㉓ 30 ÷ 6

㉔ 24 ÷ 8

㉕ 27 ÷ 3

㉖ 16 ÷ 2

㉗ 18 ÷ 6

㉘ 18 ÷ 2

㉙ 25 ÷ 5

㉚ 90 ÷ 10

㉛ 50 ÷ 10

㉜ 50 ÷ 10

㉝ 70 ÷ 10

㉞ 30 ÷ 5

㉟ 35 ÷ 5

① 50 ÷ 10

② 63 ÷ 9

③ 45 ÷ 5

④ 56 ÷ 7

⑤ 15 ÷ 3

⑥ 15 ÷ 5

⑦ 42 ÷ 6

⑧ 48 ÷ 6

⑨ 20 ÷ 10

⑩ 50 ÷ 10

⑪ 18 ÷ 6

⑫ 25 ÷ 5

⑬ 40 ÷ 10

⑭ 40 ÷ 8

⑮ 14 ÷ 7

⑯ 48 ÷ 6

⑰ 12 ÷ 6

⑱ 28 ÷ 4

⑲ 20 ÷ 10

⑳ 42 ÷ 6

㉑ 36 ÷ 6

㉒ 63 ÷ 7

㉓ 42 ÷ 6

㉔ 48 ÷ 8

㉕ 45 ÷ 9

㉖ 40 ÷ 8

㉗ 12 ÷ 4

㉘ 70 ÷ 7

㉙ 20 ÷ 4

㉚ 42 ÷ 7

㉛ 4 ÷ 2

㉜ 24 ÷ 6

㉝ 28 ÷ 7

㉞ 6 ÷ 3

㉟ 63 ÷ 9

① 35 ÷ 5

② 56 ÷ 7

③ 12 ÷ 6

④ 24 ÷ 4

⑤ 15 ÷ 5

⑥ 80 ÷ 8

⑦ 18 ÷ 2

⑧ 8 ÷ 4

⑨ 40 ÷ 4

⑩ 45 ÷ 5

⑪ 60 ÷ 6

⑫ 40 ÷ 10

⑬ 18 ÷ 3

⑭ 42 ÷ 6

⑮ 8 ÷ 4

⑯ 32 ÷ 8

⑰ 70 ÷ 7

⑱ 48 ÷ 6

⑲ 56 ÷ 8

⑳ 20 ÷ 2

㉑ 6 ÷ 2

㉒ 21 ÷ 7

㉓ 90 ÷ 9

㉔ 49 ÷ 7

㉕ 80 ÷ 8

㉖ 16 ÷ 4

㉗ 21 ÷ 7

㉘ 15 ÷ 5

㉙ 8 ÷ 2

㉚ 35 ÷ 7

㉛ 18 ÷ 6

㉜ 45 ÷ 9

㉝ 63 ÷ 7

㉞ 36 ÷ 4

㉟ 72 ÷ 8

①
  50
÷ 5

②
  20
÷ 2

③
   4
÷ 2

④
  70
÷ 10

⑤
  63
÷ 9

⑥
  40
÷ 10

⑦
  20
÷ 5

⑧
  35
÷ 5

⑨
  35
÷ 7

⑩
  54
÷ 9

⑪
  40
÷ 5

⑫
  63
÷ 7

⑬
  27
÷ 9

⑭
  10
÷ 5

⑮
  20
÷ 2

⑯
  16
÷ 8

⑰
  32
÷ 4

⑱
  40
÷ 5

⑲
  49
÷ 7

⑳
  28
÷ 4

㉑
  42
÷ 7

㉒
  20
÷ 4

㉓
  36
÷ 9

㉔
  64
÷ 8

㉕
  15
÷ 3

㉖
  21
÷ 3

㉗
  63
÷ 9

㉘
  40
÷ 4

㉙
  40
÷ 10

㉚
   6
÷ 3

㉛
  48
÷ 8

㉜
  12
÷ 3

㉝
  72
÷ 9

㉞
  36
÷ 4

㉟
  35
÷ 5

①
90
÷ 9

②
28
÷ 7

③
70
÷ 10

④
49
÷ 7

⑤
28
÷ 7

⑥
80
÷ 8

⑦
80
÷ 8

⑧
50
÷ 5

⑨
30
÷ 3

⑩
12
÷ 2

⑪
36
÷ 9

⑫
8
÷ 2

⑬
12
÷ 4

⑭
49
÷ 7

⑮
10
÷ 5

⑯
18
÷ 2

⑰
40
÷ 10

⑱
24
÷ 6

⑲
40
÷ 10

⑳
42
÷ 6

㉑
9
÷ 3

㉒
80
÷ 10

㉓
56
÷ 7

㉔
14
÷ 2

㉕
30
÷ 3

㉖
8
÷ 2

㉗
100
÷ 10

㉘
8
÷ 4

㉙
24
÷ 4

㉚
12
÷ 6

㉛
45
÷ 5

㉜
20
÷ 4

㉝
32
÷ 4

㉞
40
÷ 4

㉟
27
÷ 9

Score		Time		Worksheet 40	Name	

①	②	③	④	⑤	⑥	⑦
12 ÷ 2	80 ÷ 8	12 ÷ 2	42 ÷ 7	48 ÷ 8	100 ÷ 10	72 ÷ 8

⑧	⑨	⑩	⑪	⑫	⑬	⑭
10 ÷ 2	30 ÷ 10	63 ÷ 9	9 ÷ 3	12 ÷ 3	40 ÷ 4	16 ÷ 2

⑮	⑯	⑰	⑱	⑲	⑳	㉑
49 ÷ 7	100 ÷ 10	12 ÷ 4	12 ÷ 2	24 ÷ 4	9 ÷ 3	42 ÷ 6

㉒	㉓	㉔	㉕	㉖	㉗	㉘
40 ÷ 8	40 ÷ 8	72 ÷ 9	56 ÷ 8	48 ÷ 6	14 ÷ 2	24 ÷ 8

㉙	㉚	㉛	㉜	㉝	㉞	㉟
42 ÷ 6	14 ÷ 2	40 ÷ 10	24 ÷ 6	14 ÷ 2	90 ÷ 9	50 ÷ 5

①
56
÷ 7

②
21
÷ 3

③
30
÷ 5

④
80
÷ 8

⑤
50
÷ 5

⑥
36
÷ 4

⑦
36
÷ 4

⑧
24
÷ 8

⑨
30
÷ 10

⑩
36
÷ 9

⑪
35
÷ 7

⑫
28
÷ 7

⑬
14
÷ 2

⑭
16
÷ 4

⑮
16
÷ 4

⑯
27
÷ 3

⑰
80
÷ 8

⑱
14
÷ 7

⑲
21
÷ 7

⑳
81
÷ 9

㉑
42
÷ 6

㉒
70
÷ 10

㉓
100
÷ 10

㉔
100
÷ 10

㉕
12
÷ 2

㉖
18
÷ 6

㉗
20
÷ 10

㉘
30
÷ 5

㉙
28
÷ 4

㉚
24
÷ 8

㉛
24
÷ 3

㉜
64
÷ 8

㉝
8
÷ 2

㉞
100
÷ 10

㉟
42
÷ 7

①
$$64 \div 8$$

②
$$28 \div 4$$

③
$$18 \div 9$$

④
$$18 \div 6$$

⑤
$$30 \div 3$$

⑥
$$10 \div 5$$

⑦
$$24 \div 4$$

⑧
$$48 \div 6$$

⑨
$$48 \div 6$$

⑩
$$45 \div 5$$

⑪
$$40 \div 4$$

⑫
$$100 \div 10$$

⑬
$$90 \div 10$$

⑭
$$4 \div 2$$

⑮
$$18 \div 3$$

⑯
$$10 \div 2$$

⑰
$$40 \div 8$$

⑱
$$8 \div 4$$

⑲
$$32 \div 4$$

⑳
$$63 \div 9$$

㉑
$$16 \div 8$$

㉒
$$20 \div 2$$

㉓
$$18 \div 2$$

㉔
$$14 \div 7$$

㉕
$$12 \div 4$$

㉖
$$90 \div 10$$

㉗
$$60 \div 6$$

㉘
$$6 \div 2$$

㉙
$$42 \div 7$$

㉚
$$56 \div 7$$

㉛
$$40 \div 5$$

㉜
$$72 \div 9$$

㉝
$$15 \div 5$$

㉞
$$49 \div 7$$

㉟
$$40 \div 8$$

① 40 ÷ 4

② 10 ÷ 5

③ 70 ÷ 7

④ 18 ÷ 6

⑤ 12 ÷ 2

⑥ 12 ÷ 6

⑦ 50 ÷ 10

⑧ 50 ÷ 5

⑨ 14 ÷ 2

⑩ 30 ÷ 3

⑪ 21 ÷ 3

⑫ 80 ÷ 10

⑬ 50 ÷ 10

⑭ 14 ÷ 2

⑮ 54 ÷ 6

⑯ 50 ÷ 10

⑰ 63 ÷ 7

⑱ 54 ÷ 6

⑲ 16 ÷ 4

⑳ 50 ÷ 5

㉑ 90 ÷ 9

㉒ 36 ÷ 4

㉓ 40 ÷ 8

㉔ 48 ÷ 6

㉕ 16 ÷ 8

㉖ 35 ÷ 5

㉗ 64 ÷ 8

㉘ 48 ÷ 6

㉙ 30 ÷ 6

㉚ 20 ÷ 10

㉛ 16 ÷ 4

㉜ 10 ÷ 5

㉝ 70 ÷ 7

㉞ 32 ÷ 4

㉟ 9 ÷ 3

①
80
÷ 8

②
12
÷ 4

③
8
÷ 2

④
8
÷ 2

⑤
90
÷ 9

⑥
40
÷ 8

⑦
54
÷ 6

⑧
25
÷ 5

⑨
30
÷ 3

⑩
10
÷ 5

⑪
36
÷ 4

⑫
45
÷ 5

⑬
15
÷ 3

⑭
40
÷ 4

⑮
14
÷ 7

⑯
54
÷ 9

⑰
20
÷ 5

⑱
80
÷ 8

⑲
18
÷ 3

⑳
36
÷ 9

㉑
45
÷ 5

㉒
36
÷ 9

㉓
16
÷ 4

㉔
40
÷ 8

㉕
16
÷ 4

㉖
10
÷ 5

㉗
36
÷ 6

㉘
49
÷ 7

㉙
50
÷ 5

㉚
28
÷ 7

㉛
54
÷ 6

㉜
90
÷ 9

㉝
35
÷ 7

㉞
14
÷ 2

㉟
72
÷ 9

① 12 ÷ 4

② 21 ÷ 7

③ 8 ÷ 2

④ 27 ÷ 3

⑤ 18 ÷ 9

⑥ 20 ÷ 10

⑦ 35 ÷ 7

⑧ 18 ÷ 9

⑨ 20 ÷ 2

⑩ 30 ÷ 3

⑪ 64 ÷ 8

⑫ 35 ÷ 7

⑬ 24 ÷ 4

⑭ 20 ÷ 2

⑮ 32 ÷ 8

⑯ 24 ÷ 6

⑰ 40 ÷ 10

⑱ 20 ÷ 10

⑲ 14 ÷ 2

⑳ 42 ÷ 7

㉑ 35 ÷ 7

㉒ 12 ÷ 2

㉓ 35 ÷ 5

㉔ 30 ÷ 3

㉕ 42 ÷ 6

㉖ 80 ÷ 10

㉗ 60 ÷ 10

㉘ 18 ÷ 9

㉙ 40 ÷ 10

㉚ 14 ÷ 2

㉛ 72 ÷ 8

㉜ 36 ÷ 9

㉝ 24 ÷ 6

㉞ 70 ÷ 10

㉟ 12 ÷ 4

① 54 ÷ 9

② 45 ÷ 9

③ 45 ÷ 9

④ 54 ÷ 6

⑤ 80 ÷ 10

⑥ 12 ÷ 2

⑦ 18 ÷ 2

⑧ 48 ÷ 8

⑨ 90 ÷ 9

⑩ 27 ÷ 9

⑪ 24 ÷ 4

⑫ 45 ÷ 9

⑬ 54 ÷ 9

⑭ 18 ÷ 9

⑮ 14 ÷ 2

⑯ 49 ÷ 7

⑰ 45 ÷ 5

⑱ 24 ÷ 3

⑲ 16 ÷ 8

⑳ 56 ÷ 7

㉑ 70 ÷ 10

㉒ 100 ÷ 10

㉓ 32 ÷ 8

㉔ 40 ÷ 5

㉕ 18 ÷ 9

㉖ 15 ÷ 3

㉗ 24 ÷ 4

㉘ 12 ÷ 6

㉙ 54 ÷ 6

㉚ 18 ÷ 3

㉛ 4 ÷ 2

㉜ 28 ÷ 4

㉝ 48 ÷ 8

㉞ 81 ÷ 9

㉟ 28 ÷ 7

①
42
÷ 6

②
8
÷ 2

③
10
÷ 5

④
6
÷ 2

⑤
81
÷ 9

⑥
54
÷ 6

⑦
49
÷ 7

⑧
56
÷ 7

⑨
40
÷ 8

⑩
16
÷ 4

⑪
72
÷ 8

⑫
20
÷ 4

⑬
16
÷ 8

⑭
60
÷ 10

⑮
36
÷ 6

⑯
32
÷ 4

⑰
72
÷ 8

⑱
8
÷ 2

⑲
90
÷ 9

⑳
16
÷ 2

㉑
12
÷ 2

㉒
56
÷ 7

㉓
20
÷ 5

㉔
27
÷ 3

㉕
80
÷ 10

㉖
72
÷ 9

㉗
20
÷ 4

㉘
72
÷ 8

㉙
63
÷ 9

㉚
10
÷ 5

㉛
35
÷ 7

㉜
16
÷ 2

㉝
30
÷ 3

㉞
64
÷ 8

㉟
6
÷ 2

① 49 ÷ 7

② 21 ÷ 3

③ 42 ÷ 6

④ 8 ÷ 2

⑤ 80 ÷ 8

⑥ 25 ÷ 5

⑦ 18 ÷ 6

⑧ 60 ÷ 6

⑨ 40 ÷ 10

⑩ 10 ÷ 2

⑪ 27 ÷ 3

⑫ 14 ÷ 7

⑬ 12 ÷ 2

⑭ 48 ÷ 6

⑮ 20 ÷ 4

⑯ 80 ÷ 8

⑰ 10 ÷ 2

⑱ 15 ÷ 5

⑲ 42 ÷ 6

⑳ 15 ÷ 5

㉑ 28 ÷ 7

㉒ 24 ÷ 6

㉓ 20 ÷ 2

㉔ 80 ÷ 10

㉕ 24 ÷ 8

㉖ 45 ÷ 9

㉗ 18 ÷ 6

㉘ 64 ÷ 8

㉙ 8 ÷ 2

㉚ 100 ÷ 10

㉛ 18 ÷ 9

㉜ 50 ÷ 5

㉝ 40 ÷ 5

㉞ 21 ÷ 7

㉟ 56 ÷ 8

① 20 ÷ 4

② 20 ÷ 10

③ 18 ÷ 2

④ 30 ÷ 6

⑤ 6 ÷ 3

⑥ 30 ÷ 5

⑦ 24 ÷ 6

⑧ 54 ÷ 9

⑨ 24 ÷ 6

⑩ 63 ÷ 7

⑪ 80 ÷ 10

⑫ 63 ÷ 7

⑬ 16 ÷ 2

⑭ 63 ÷ 7

⑮ 90 ÷ 10

⑯ 60 ÷ 6

⑰ 12 ÷ 6

⑱ 15 ÷ 3

⑲ 18 ÷ 3

⑳ 16 ÷ 2

㉑ 30 ÷ 3

㉒ 42 ÷ 6

㉓ 28 ÷ 4

㉔ 32 ÷ 8

㉕ 63 ÷ 7

㉖ 100 ÷ 10

㉗ 12 ÷ 4

㉘ 45 ÷ 9

㉙ 20 ÷ 10

㉚ 63 ÷ 7

㉛ 16 ÷ 2

㉜ 64 ÷ 8

㉝ 35 ÷ 7

㉞ 72 ÷ 8

㉟ 24 ÷ 6

①
$$24 \div 3$$

②
$$54 \div 9$$

③
$$20 \div 2$$

④
$$15 \div 5$$

⑤
$$21 \div 3$$

⑥
$$6 \div 2$$

⑦
$$4 \div 2$$

⑧
$$50 \div 10$$

⑨
$$56 \div 7$$

⑩
$$80 \div 8$$

⑪
$$40 \div 5$$

⑫
$$12 \div 3$$

⑬
$$63 \div 9$$

⑭
$$20 \div 2$$

⑮
$$54 \div 6$$

⑯
$$20 \div 5$$

⑰
$$32 \div 4$$

⑱
$$10 \div 5$$

⑲
$$30 \div 10$$

⑳
$$49 \div 7$$

㉑
$$18 \div 3$$

㉒
$$24 \div 3$$

㉓
$$81 \div 9$$

㉔
$$40 \div 10$$

㉕
$$42 \div 6$$

㉖
$$72 \div 9$$

㉗
$$48 \div 6$$

㉘
$$80 \div 10$$

㉙
$$40 \div 5$$

㉚
$$49 \div 7$$

㉛
$$14 \div 7$$

㉜
$$16 \div 2$$

㉝
$$45 \div 5$$

㉞
$$4 \div 2$$

㉟
$$18 \div 3$$

①
$$44 \div 11$$

②
$$110 \div 11$$

③
$$110 \div 11$$

④
$$33 \div 11$$

⑤
$$121 \div 11$$

⑥
$$132 \div 11$$

⑦
$$77 \div 11$$

⑧
$$132 \div 11$$

⑨
$$22 \div 11$$

⑩
$$132 \div 11$$

⑪
$$110 \div 11$$

⑫
$$121 \div 11$$

⑬
$$0 \div 11$$

⑭
$$121 \div 11$$

⑮
$$66 \div 11$$

⑯
$$121 \div 11$$

⑰
$$0 \div 11$$

⑱
$$33 \div 11$$

⑲
$$88 \div 11$$

⑳
$$0 \div 11$$

㉑
$$11 \div 11$$

㉒
$$88 \div 11$$

㉓
$$99 \div 11$$

㉔
$$110 \div 11$$

㉕
$$110 \div 11$$

㉖
$$77 \div 11$$

㉗
$$33 \div 11$$

㉘
$$44 \div 11$$

㉙
$$33 \div 11$$

㉚
$$132 \div 11$$

㉛
$$88 \div 11$$

㉜
$$121 \div 11$$

㉝
$$33 \div 11$$

㉞
$$22 \div 11$$

㉟
$$66 \div 11$$

① 66 ÷ 11

② 55 ÷ 11

③ 99 ÷ 11

④ 22 ÷ 11

⑤ 99 ÷ 11

⑥ 88 ÷ 11

⑦ 132 ÷ 11

⑧ 110 ÷ 11

⑨ 33 ÷ 11

⑩ 99 ÷ 11

⑪ 44 ÷ 11

⑫ 22 ÷ 11

⑬ 132 ÷ 11

⑭ 121 ÷ 11

⑮ 88 ÷ 11

⑯ 0 ÷ 11

⑰ 55 ÷ 11

⑱ 44 ÷ 11

⑲ 55 ÷ 11

⑳ 88 ÷ 11

㉑ 110 ÷ 11

㉒ 66 ÷ 11

㉓ 0 ÷ 11

㉔ 132 ÷ 11

㉕ 121 ÷ 11

㉖ 22 ÷ 11

㉗ 132 ÷ 11

㉘ 33 ÷ 11

㉙ 22 ÷ 11

㉚ 0 ÷ 11

㉛ 110 ÷ 11

㉜ 110 ÷ 11

㉝ 44 ÷ 11

㉞ 0 ÷ 11

㉟ 88 ÷ 11

①
22
÷ 11

②
22
÷ 11

③
66
÷ 11

④
44
÷ 11

⑤
44
÷ 11

⑥
11
÷ 11

⑦
55
÷ 11

⑧
132
÷ 11

⑨
88
÷ 11

⑩
66
÷ 11

⑪
77
÷ 11

⑫
44
÷ 11

⑬
88
÷ 11

⑭
22
÷ 11

⑮
88
÷ 11

⑯
77
÷ 11

⑰
33
÷ 11

⑱
33
÷ 11

⑲
22
÷ 11

⑳
99
÷ 11

㉑
110
÷ 11

㉒
77
÷ 11

㉓
121
÷ 11

㉔
44
÷ 11

㉕
88
÷ 11

㉖
44
÷ 11

㉗
44
÷ 11

㉘
11
÷ 11

㉙
132
÷ 11

㉚
77
÷ 11

㉛
11
÷ 11

㉜
132
÷ 11

㉝
33
÷ 11

㉞
132
÷ 11

㉟
11
÷ 11

① 99 ÷ 11

② 132 ÷ 11

③ 0 ÷ 11

④ 11 ÷ 11

⑤ 88 ÷ 11

⑥ 99 ÷ 11

⑦ 99 ÷ 11

⑧ 11 ÷ 11

⑨ 33 ÷ 11

⑩ 88 ÷ 11

⑪ 44 ÷ 11

⑫ 11 ÷ 11

⑬ 121 ÷ 11

⑭ 110 ÷ 11

⑮ 22 ÷ 11

⑯ 33 ÷ 11

⑰ 66 ÷ 11

⑱ 55 ÷ 11

⑲ 121 ÷ 11

⑳ 22 ÷ 11

㉑ 110 ÷ 11

㉒ 99 ÷ 11

㉓ 33 ÷ 11

㉔ 0 ÷ 11

㉕ 33 ÷ 11

㉖ 11 ÷ 11

㉗ 121 ÷ 11

㉘ 33 ÷ 11

㉙ 22 ÷ 11

㉚ 132 ÷ 11

㉛ 132 ÷ 11

㉜ 99 ÷ 11

㉝ 22 ÷ 11

㉞ 22 ÷ 11

㉟ 77 ÷ 11

①
99
÷ 11

②
66
÷ 11

③
44
÷ 11

④
99
÷ 11

⑤
77
÷ 11

⑥
44
÷ 11

⑦
132
÷ 11

⑧
66
÷ 11

⑨
77
÷ 11

⑩
44
÷ 11

⑪
44
÷ 11

⑫
55
÷ 11

⑬
55
÷ 11

⑭
66
÷ 11

⑮
66
÷ 11

⑯
77
÷ 11

⑰
88
÷ 11

⑱
88
÷ 11

⑲
121
÷ 11

⑳
77
÷ 11

㉑
22
÷ 11

㉒
121
÷ 11

㉓
132
÷ 11

㉔
22
÷ 11

㉕
44
÷ 11

㉖
44
÷ 11

㉗
110
÷ 11

㉘
66
÷ 11

㉙
121
÷ 11

㉚
66
÷ 11

㉛
22
÷ 11

㉜
99
÷ 11

㉝
88
÷ 11

㉞
0
÷ 11

㉟
66
÷ 11

① 120 ÷ 12

② 120 ÷ 12

③ 0 ÷ 12

④ 144 ÷ 12

⑤ 84 ÷ 12

⑥ 24 ÷ 12

⑦ 60 ÷ 12

⑧ 144 ÷ 12

⑨ 72 ÷ 12

⑩ 84 ÷ 12

⑪ 12 ÷ 12

⑫ 84 ÷ 12

⑬ 36 ÷ 12

⑭ 96 ÷ 12

⑮ 120 ÷ 12

⑯ 24 ÷ 12

⑰ 72 ÷ 12

⑱ 96 ÷ 12

⑲ 12 ÷ 12

⑳ 132 ÷ 12

㉑ 144 ÷ 12

㉒ 120 ÷ 12

㉓ 132 ÷ 12

㉔ 0 ÷ 12

㉕ 12 ÷ 12

㉖ 96 ÷ 12

㉗ 36 ÷ 12

㉘ 96 ÷ 12

㉙ 12 ÷ 12

㉚ 0 ÷ 12

㉛ 108 ÷ 12

㉜ 84 ÷ 12

㉝ 60 ÷ 12

㉞ 12 ÷ 12

㉟ 48 ÷ 12

① 144 ÷ 12

② 24 ÷ 12

③ 84 ÷ 12

④ 36 ÷ 12

⑤ 132 ÷ 12

⑥ 36 ÷ 12

⑦ 72 ÷ 12

⑧ 0 ÷ 12

⑨ 0 ÷ 12

⑩ 72 ÷ 12

⑪ 132 ÷ 12

⑫ 12 ÷ 12

⑬ 108 ÷ 12

⑭ 24 ÷ 12

⑮ 0 ÷ 12

⑯ 60 ÷ 12

⑰ 72 ÷ 12

⑱ 72 ÷ 12

⑲ 48 ÷ 12

⑳ 36 ÷ 12

㉑ 12 ÷ 12

㉒ 84 ÷ 12

㉓ 36 ÷ 12

㉔ 12 ÷ 12

㉕ 24 ÷ 12

㉖ 24 ÷ 12

㉗ 132 ÷ 12

㉘ 0 ÷ 12

㉙ 72 ÷ 12

㉚ 96 ÷ 12

㉛ 96 ÷ 12

㉜ 84 ÷ 12

㉝ 24 ÷ 12

㉞ 48 ÷ 12

㉟ 24 ÷ 12

Score		Time		Worksheet 58	Name	

① 36 ÷ 12	② 60 ÷ 12	③ 0 ÷ 12	④ 84 ÷ 12	⑤ 0 ÷ 12	⑥ 48 ÷ 12	⑦ 72 ÷ 12
⑧ 108 ÷ 12	⑨ 60 ÷ 12	⑩ 108 ÷ 12	⑪ 0 ÷ 12	⑫ 144 ÷ 12	⑬ 48 ÷ 12	⑭ 60 ÷ 12
⑮ 108 ÷ 12	⑯ 60 ÷ 12	⑰ 60 ÷ 12	⑱ 72 ÷ 12	⑲ 144 ÷ 12	⑳ 84 ÷ 12	㉑ 24 ÷ 12
㉒ 72 ÷ 12	㉓ 132 ÷ 12	㉔ 84 ÷ 12	㉕ 84 ÷ 12	㉖ 48 ÷ 12	㉗ 132 ÷ 12	㉘ 0 ÷ 12
㉙ 48 ÷ 12	㉚ 144 ÷ 12	㉛ 120 ÷ 12	㉜ 120 ÷ 12	㉝ 72 ÷ 12	㉞ 84 ÷ 12	㉟ 144 ÷ 12

①
$$0 \div 12$$

②
$$12 \div 12$$

③
$$72 \div 12$$

④
$$132 \div 12$$

⑤
$$60 \div 12$$

⑥
$$132 \div 12$$

⑦
$$108 \div 12$$

⑧
$$48 \div 12$$

⑨
$$108 \div 12$$

⑩
$$144 \div 12$$

⑪
$$132 \div 12$$

⑫
$$84 \div 12$$

⑬
$$84 \div 12$$

⑭
$$108 \div 12$$

⑮
$$0 \div 12$$

⑯
$$96 \div 12$$

⑰
$$12 \div 12$$

⑱
$$72 \div 12$$

⑲
$$72 \div 12$$

⑳
$$48 \div 12$$

㉑
$$60 \div 12$$

㉒
$$24 \div 12$$

㉓
$$84 \div 12$$

㉔
$$84 \div 12$$

㉕
$$36 \div 12$$

㉖
$$0 \div 12$$

㉗
$$120 \div 12$$

㉘
$$84 \div 12$$

㉙
$$60 \div 12$$

㉚
$$36 \div 12$$

㉛
$$72 \div 12$$

㉜
$$60 \div 12$$

㉝
$$84 \div 12$$

㉞
$$24 \div 12$$

㉟
$$36 \div 12$$

①
96
÷ 12

②
72
÷ 12

③
84
÷ 12

④
60
÷ 12

⑤
120
÷ 12

⑥
36
÷ 12

⑦
120
÷ 12

⑧
0
÷ 12

⑨
0
÷ 12

⑩
96
÷ 12

⑪
36
÷ 12

⑫
60
÷ 12

⑬
144
÷ 12

⑭
12
÷ 12

⑮
24
÷ 12

⑯
108
÷ 12

⑰
144
÷ 12

⑱
48
÷ 12

⑲
12
÷ 12

⑳
120
÷ 12

㉑
132
÷ 12

㉒
120
÷ 12

㉓
24
÷ 12

㉔
84
÷ 12

㉕
36
÷ 12

㉖
144
÷ 12

㉗
60
÷ 12

㉘
48
÷ 12

㉙
108
÷ 12

㉚
0
÷ 12

㉛
60
÷ 12

㉜
84
÷ 12

㉝
24
÷ 12

㉞
108
÷ 12

㉟
96
÷ 12

① 12 ÷ 12

② 77 ÷ 11

③ 55 ÷ 5

④ 12 ÷ 1

⑤ 0 ÷ 11

⑥ 108 ÷ 12

⑦ 80 ÷ 10

⑧ 72 ÷ 6

⑨ 108 ÷ 12

⑩ 66 ÷ 6

⑪ 6 ÷ 2

⑫ 45 ÷ 5

⑬ 88 ÷ 11

⑭ 35 ÷ 7

⑮ 48 ÷ 8

⑯ 20 ÷ 2

⑰ 25 ÷ 5

⑱ 2 ÷ 2

⑲ 90 ÷ 10

⑳ 21 ÷ 7

㉑ 8 ÷ 4

㉒ 16 ÷ 8

㉓ 44 ÷ 4

㉔ 10 ÷ 10

㉕ 12 ÷ 3

㉖ 40 ÷ 10

㉗ 18 ÷ 2

㉘ 0 ÷ 6

㉙ 35 ÷ 7

㉚ 12 ÷ 3

㉛ 120 ÷ 12

㉜ 12 ÷ 3

㉝ 5 ÷ 1

㉞ 132 ÷ 12

㉟ 72 ÷ 9

①
$$132 \div 11$$

②
$$42 \div 6$$

③
$$84 \div 12$$

④
$$30 \div 3$$

⑤
$$33 \div 11$$

⑥
$$35 \div 7$$

⑦
$$15 \div 3$$

⑧
$$72 \div 8$$

⑨
$$20 \div 10$$

⑩
$$7 \div 1$$

⑪
$$4 \div 4$$

⑫
$$120 \div 10$$

⑬
$$0 \div 7$$

⑭
$$30 \div 3$$

⑮
$$63 \div 9$$

⑯
$$81 \div 9$$

⑰
$$63 \div 9$$

⑱
$$96 \div 12$$

⑲
$$36 \div 12$$

⑳
$$20 \div 10$$

㉑
$$44 \div 11$$

㉒
$$9 \div 1$$

㉓
$$0 \div 5$$

㉔
$$54 \div 9$$

㉕
$$12 \div 6$$

㉖
$$99 \div 11$$

㉗
$$12 \div 2$$

㉘
$$48 \div 12$$

㉙
$$44 \div 11$$

㉚
$$132 \div 11$$

㉛
$$48 \div 8$$

㉜
$$6 \div 1$$

㉝
$$14 \div 2$$

㉞
$$0 \div 1$$

㉟
$$60 \div 12$$

① 63 ÷ 7

② 3 ÷ 1

③ 35 ÷ 5

④ 11 ÷ 11

⑤ 20 ÷ 10

⑥ 96 ÷ 12

⑦ 10 ÷ 5

⑧ 0 ÷ 8

⑨ 40 ÷ 10

⑩ 36 ÷ 3

⑪ 12 ÷ 2

⑫ 108 ÷ 12

⑬ 63 ÷ 7

⑭ 7 ÷ 1

⑮ 60 ÷ 12

⑯ 70 ÷ 7

⑰ 3 ÷ 1

⑱ 48 ÷ 6

⑲ 30 ÷ 5

⑳ 0 ÷ 4

㉑ 80 ÷ 10

㉒ 7 ÷ 1

㉓ 110 ÷ 10

㉔ 35 ÷ 7

㉕ 3 ÷ 3

㉖ 63 ÷ 9

㉗ 0 ÷ 8

㉘ 22 ÷ 2

㉙ 30 ÷ 6

㉚ 22 ÷ 2

㉛ 72 ÷ 12

㉜ 16 ÷ 2

㉝ 7 ÷ 1

㉞ 45 ÷ 9

㉟ 10 ÷ 1

①
$$36 \div 3$$

②
$$0 \div 9$$

③
$$77 \div 7$$

④
$$18 \div 6$$

⑤
$$30 \div 10$$

⑥
$$30 \div 6$$

⑦
$$16 \div 2$$

⑧
$$90 \div 9$$

⑨
$$9 \div 9$$

⑩
$$27 \div 3$$

⑪
$$44 \div 4$$

⑫
$$35 \div 7$$

⑬
$$28 \div 4$$

⑭
$$36 \div 12$$

⑮
$$45 \div 9$$

⑯
$$6 \div 6$$

⑰
$$48 \div 6$$

⑱
$$55 \div 5$$

⑲
$$81 \div 9$$

⑳
$$70 \div 10$$

㉑
$$4 \div 2$$

㉒
$$100 \div 10$$

㉓
$$0 \div 6$$

㉔
$$18 \div 2$$

㉕
$$63 \div 9$$

㉖
$$18 \div 6$$

㉗
$$0 \div 5$$

㉘
$$120 \div 10$$

㉙
$$10 \div 2$$

㉚
$$55 \div 11$$

㉛
$$10 \div 10$$

㉜
$$60 \div 5$$

㉝
$$72 \div 8$$

㉞
$$40 \div 8$$

㉟
$$28 \div 7$$

① 99 ÷ 11

② 18 ÷ 6

③ 90 ÷ 10

④ 6 ÷ 6

⑤ 24 ÷ 4

⑥ 84 ÷ 12

⑦ 12 ÷ 12

⑧ 5 ÷ 5

⑨ 60 ÷ 6

⑩ 8 ÷ 8

⑪ 12 ÷ 4

⑫ 40 ÷ 10

⑬ 27 ÷ 3

⑭ 0 ÷ 11

⑮ 10 ÷ 5

⑯ 24 ÷ 4

⑰ 88 ÷ 11

⑱ 0 ÷ 3

⑲ 48 ÷ 6

⑳ 72 ÷ 12

㉑ 20 ÷ 2

㉒ 6 ÷ 6

㉓ 66 ÷ 6

㉔ 40 ÷ 5

㉕ 40 ÷ 4

㉖ 36 ÷ 4

㉗ 9 ÷ 3

㉘ 0 ÷ 1

㉙ 66 ÷ 6

㉚ 63 ÷ 9

㉛ 3 ÷ 1

㉜ 48 ÷ 6

㉝ 25 ÷ 5

㉞ 80 ÷ 8

㉟ 11 ÷ 11

①
4
÷ 2

②
55
÷ 11

③
12
÷ 4

④
80
÷ 8

⑤
45
÷ 9

⑥
0
÷ 11

⑦
9
÷ 1

⑧
0
÷ 12

⑨
16
÷ 4

⑩
96
÷ 8

⑪
108
÷ 12

⑫
24
÷ 2

⑬
77
÷ 7

⑭
10
÷ 5

⑮
2
÷ 1

⑯
70
÷ 10

⑰
0
÷ 10

⑱
100
÷ 10

⑲
0
÷ 10

⑳
20
÷ 10

㉑
132
÷ 12

㉒
6
÷ 6

㉓
6
÷ 2

㉔
0
÷ 6

㉕
108
÷ 9

㉖
14
÷ 7

㉗
0
÷ 2

㉘
15
÷ 3

㉙
8
÷ 4

㉚
24
÷ 4

㉛
0
÷ 7

㉜
24
÷ 2

㉝
36
÷ 9

㉞
24
÷ 2

㉟
10
÷ 2

① 24 ÷ 12

② 42 ÷ 7

③ 80 ÷ 8

④ 60 ÷ 12

⑤ 27 ÷ 9

⑥ 72 ÷ 9

⑦ 28 ÷ 7

⑧ 24 ÷ 12

⑨ 120 ÷ 10

⑩ 60 ÷ 10

⑪ 3 ÷ 3

⑫ 10 ÷ 2

⑬ 36 ÷ 3

⑭ 11 ÷ 11

⑮ 5 ÷ 5

⑯ 14 ÷ 2

⑰ 7 ÷ 1

⑱ 7 ÷ 7

⑲ 40 ÷ 10

⑳ 80 ÷ 8

㉑ 9 ÷ 1

㉒ 36 ÷ 12

㉓ 60 ÷ 5

㉔ 24 ÷ 4

㉕ 12 ÷ 6

㉖ 63 ÷ 9

㉗ 6 ÷ 2

㉘ 96 ÷ 8

㉙ 11 ÷ 11

㉚ 11 ÷ 11

㉛ 10 ÷ 5

㉜ 12 ÷ 1

㉝ 14 ÷ 7

㉞ 10 ÷ 5

㉟ 24 ÷ 12

① 144 ÷ 12

② 88 ÷ 8

③ 10 ÷ 10

④ 77 ÷ 11

⑤ 35 ÷ 5

⑥ 24 ÷ 8

⑦ 110 ÷ 10

⑧ 108 ÷ 12

⑨ 2 ÷ 2

⑩ 14 ÷ 2

⑪ 84 ÷ 7

⑫ 33 ÷ 11

⑬ 24 ÷ 12

⑭ 48 ÷ 6

⑮ 32 ÷ 8

⑯ 33 ÷ 3

⑰ 120 ÷ 10

⑱ 9 ÷ 9

⑲ 54 ÷ 6

⑳ 24 ÷ 12

㉑ 32 ÷ 4

㉒ 11 ÷ 1

㉓ 27 ÷ 3

㉔ 24 ÷ 4

㉕ 49 ÷ 7

㉖ 32 ÷ 4

㉗ 90 ÷ 9

㉘ 10 ÷ 1

㉙ 9 ÷ 3

㉚ 24 ÷ 3

㉛ 56 ÷ 7

㉜ 0 ÷ 4

㉝ 40 ÷ 10

㉞ 100 ÷ 10

㉟ 21 ÷ 3

①
$$12 \div 6$$

②
$$7 \div 7$$

③
$$40 \div 5$$

④
$$66 \div 11$$

⑤
$$2 \div 2$$

⑥
$$64 \div 8$$

⑦
$$32 \div 4$$

⑧
$$0 \div 6$$

⑨
$$60 \div 10$$

⑩
$$72 \div 6$$

⑪
$$144 \div 12$$

⑫
$$72 \div 6$$

⑬
$$0 \div 7$$

⑭
$$84 \div 12$$

⑮
$$32 \div 4$$

⑯
$$90 \div 9$$

⑰
$$99 \div 11$$

⑱
$$42 \div 6$$

⑲
$$7 \div 7$$

⑳
$$84 \div 7$$

㉑
$$16 \div 4$$

㉒
$$132 \div 12$$

㉓
$$77 \div 7$$

㉔
$$30 \div 10$$

㉕
$$8 \div 1$$

㉖
$$27 \div 3$$

㉗
$$36 \div 3$$

㉘
$$33 \div 11$$

㉙
$$99 \div 11$$

㉚
$$0 \div 5$$

㉛
$$33 \div 3$$

㉜
$$24 \div 12$$

㉝
$$36 \div 9$$

㉞
$$77 \div 7$$

㉟
$$54 \div 9$$

①
$$12 \div 3$$

②
$$10 \div 5$$

③
$$99 \div 11$$

④
$$0 \div 3$$

⑤
$$14 \div 7$$

⑥
$$1 \div 1$$

⑦
$$0 \div 2$$

⑧
$$77 \div 11$$

⑨
$$10 \div 1$$

⑩
$$66 \div 11$$

⑪
$$60 \div 12$$

⑫
$$45 \div 9$$

⑬
$$36 \div 6$$

⑭
$$12 \div 6$$

⑮
$$5 \div 5$$

⑯
$$40 \div 5$$

⑰
$$96 \div 12$$

⑱
$$0 \div 6$$

⑲
$$56 \div 8$$

⑳
$$5 \div 1$$

㉑
$$10 \div 1$$

㉒
$$27 \div 9$$

㉓
$$10 \div 2$$

㉔
$$36 \div 6$$

㉕
$$63 \div 7$$

㉖
$$12 \div 1$$

㉗
$$84 \div 7$$

㉘
$$35 \div 7$$

㉙
$$0 \div 10$$

㉚
$$33 \div 3$$

㉛
$$0 \div 3$$

㉜
$$24 \div 12$$

㉝
$$9 \div 3$$

㉞
$$55 \div 11$$

㉟
$$0 \div 6$$

① 110 ÷ 11

② 18 ÷ 3

③ 110 ÷ 11

④ 72 ÷ 6

⑤ 27 ÷ 3

⑥ 35 ÷ 5

⑦ 12 ÷ 4

⑧ 70 ÷ 10

⑨ 63 ÷ 7

⑩ 16 ÷ 4

⑪ 70 ÷ 10

⑫ 96 ÷ 12

⑬ 56 ÷ 8

⑭ 14 ÷ 2

⑮ 120 ÷ 12

⑯ 42 ÷ 7

⑰ 30 ÷ 10

⑱ 72 ÷ 8

⑲ 45 ÷ 9

⑳ 30 ÷ 3

㉑ 48 ÷ 6

㉒ 24 ÷ 6

㉓ 96 ÷ 8

㉔ 60 ÷ 6

㉕ 18 ÷ 2

㉖ 24 ÷ 4

㉗ 8 ÷ 4

㉘ 40 ÷ 4

㉙ 48 ÷ 4

㉚ 72 ÷ 9

㉛ 18 ÷ 2

㉜ 72 ÷ 8

㉝ 42 ÷ 7

㉞ 20 ÷ 5

㉟ 4 ÷ 2

① 40 ÷ 10

② 18 ÷ 6

③ 55 ÷ 11

④ 42 ÷ 7

⑤ 33 ÷ 3

⑥ 27 ÷ 9

⑦ 120 ÷ 10

⑧ 60 ÷ 6

⑨ 8 ÷ 4

⑩ 32 ÷ 4

⑪ 70 ÷ 10

⑫ 70 ÷ 7

⑬ 21 ÷ 7

⑭ 44 ÷ 4

⑮ 40 ÷ 10

⑯ 60 ÷ 10

⑰ 28 ÷ 7

⑱ 33 ÷ 3

⑲ 24 ÷ 12

⑳ 88 ÷ 8

㉑ 108 ÷ 12

㉒ 54 ÷ 6

㉓ 90 ÷ 10

㉔ 60 ÷ 12

㉕ 90 ÷ 10

㉖ 24 ÷ 4

㉗ 84 ÷ 12

㉘ 72 ÷ 8

㉙ 60 ÷ 12

㉚ 54 ÷ 6

㉛ 80 ÷ 10

㉜ 20 ÷ 10

㉝ 84 ÷ 12

㉞ 16 ÷ 2

㉟ 36 ÷ 9

①
48
÷ 6

②
33
÷ 3

③
99
÷ 9

④
99
÷ 9

⑤
12
÷ 3

⑥
16
÷ 4

⑦
36
÷ 12

⑧
36
÷ 4

⑨
48
÷ 8

⑩
30
÷ 10

⑪
15
÷ 3

⑫
16
÷ 8

⑬
36
÷ 4

⑭
24
÷ 2

⑮
12
÷ 4

⑯
9
÷ 3

⑰
55
÷ 5

⑱
72
÷ 9

⑲
20
÷ 2

⑳
35
÷ 5

㉑
55
÷ 11

㉒
90
÷ 9

㉓
108
÷ 9

㉔
12
÷ 2

㉕
54
÷ 6

㉖
60
÷ 6

㉗
36
÷ 3

㉘
14
÷ 7

㉙
60
÷ 12

㉚
35
÷ 5

㉛
63
÷ 7

㉜
44
÷ 11

㉝
63
÷ 7

㉞
48
÷ 12

㉟
16
÷ 2

①
$$\begin{array}{r} 50 \\ \div\ 5 \\ \hline \end{array}$$

②
$$\begin{array}{r} 60 \\ \div\ 10 \\ \hline \end{array}$$

③
$$\begin{array}{r} 84 \\ \div\ 7 \\ \hline \end{array}$$

④
$$\begin{array}{r} 54 \\ \div\ 9 \\ \hline \end{array}$$

⑤
$$\begin{array}{r} 60 \\ \div\ 5 \\ \hline \end{array}$$

⑥
$$\begin{array}{r} 4 \\ \div\ 2 \\ \hline \end{array}$$

⑦
$$\begin{array}{r} 81 \\ \div\ 9 \\ \hline \end{array}$$

⑧
$$\begin{array}{r} 24 \\ \div\ 3 \\ \hline \end{array}$$

⑨
$$\begin{array}{r} 55 \\ \div\ 11 \\ \hline \end{array}$$

⑩
$$\begin{array}{r} 20 \\ \div\ 5 \\ \hline \end{array}$$

⑪
$$\begin{array}{r} 12 \\ \div\ 4 \\ \hline \end{array}$$

⑫
$$\begin{array}{r} 72 \\ \div\ 9 \\ \hline \end{array}$$

⑬
$$\begin{array}{r} 28 \\ \div\ 4 \\ \hline \end{array}$$

⑭
$$\begin{array}{r} 48 \\ \div\ 8 \\ \hline \end{array}$$

⑮
$$\begin{array}{r} 72 \\ \div\ 8 \\ \hline \end{array}$$

⑯
$$\begin{array}{r} 8 \\ \div\ 4 \\ \hline \end{array}$$

⑰
$$\begin{array}{r} 144 \\ \div\ 12 \\ \hline \end{array}$$

⑱
$$\begin{array}{r} 24 \\ \div\ 4 \\ \hline \end{array}$$

⑲
$$\begin{array}{r} 28 \\ \div\ 7 \\ \hline \end{array}$$

⑳
$$\begin{array}{r} 36 \\ \div\ 4 \\ \hline \end{array}$$

㉑
$$\begin{array}{r} 36 \\ \div\ 4 \\ \hline \end{array}$$

㉒
$$\begin{array}{r} 48 \\ \div\ 8 \\ \hline \end{array}$$

㉓
$$\begin{array}{r} 18 \\ \div\ 9 \\ \hline \end{array}$$

㉔
$$\begin{array}{r} 40 \\ \div\ 5 \\ \hline \end{array}$$

㉕
$$\begin{array}{r} 30 \\ \div\ 5 \\ \hline \end{array}$$

㉖
$$\begin{array}{r} 132 \\ \div\ 12 \\ \hline \end{array}$$

㉗
$$\begin{array}{r} 24 \\ \div\ 12 \\ \hline \end{array}$$

㉘
$$\begin{array}{r} 24 \\ \div\ 12 \\ \hline \end{array}$$

㉙
$$\begin{array}{r} 27 \\ \div\ 3 \\ \hline \end{array}$$

㉚
$$\begin{array}{r} 96 \\ \div\ 12 \\ \hline \end{array}$$

㉛
$$\begin{array}{r} 14 \\ \div\ 7 \\ \hline \end{array}$$

㉜
$$\begin{array}{r} 36 \\ \div\ 3 \\ \hline \end{array}$$

㉝
$$\begin{array}{r} 90 \\ \div\ 10 \\ \hline \end{array}$$

㉞
$$\begin{array}{r} 20 \\ \div\ 10 \\ \hline \end{array}$$

㉟
$$\begin{array}{r} 72 \\ \div\ 6 \\ \hline \end{array}$$

①
48
÷ 6

②
24
÷ 3

③
72
÷ 6

④
96
÷ 12

⑤
49
÷ 7

⑥
90
÷ 9

⑦
72
÷ 8

⑧
60
÷ 5

⑨
70
÷ 10

⑩
54
÷ 9

⑪
48
÷ 4

⑫
42
÷ 7

⑬
77
÷ 11

⑭
12
÷ 4

⑮
60
÷ 6

⑯
6
÷ 3

⑰
36
÷ 12

⑱
49
÷ 7

⑲
27
÷ 3

⑳
40
÷ 5

㉑
25
÷ 5

㉒
32
÷ 8

㉓
50
÷ 10

㉔
132
÷ 12

㉕
49
÷ 7

㉖
36
÷ 4

㉗
14
÷ 7

㉘
72
÷ 12

㉙
40
÷ 4

㉚
90
÷ 10

㉛
110
÷ 11

㉜
90
÷ 10

㉝
60
÷ 12

㉞
28
÷ 4

㉟
8
÷ 4

①
108
÷ 9

②
108
÷ 12

③
60
÷ 5

④
84
÷ 7

⑤
63
÷ 7

⑥
24
÷ 8

⑦
24
÷ 6

⑧
88
÷ 11

⑨
16
÷ 4

⑩
96
÷ 12

⑪
63
÷ 7

⑫
16
÷ 8

⑬
99
÷ 9

⑭
30
÷ 3

⑮
60
÷ 5

⑯
90
÷ 9

⑰
96
÷ 8

⑱
132
÷ 12

⑲
16
÷ 4

⑳
70
÷ 10

㉑
42
÷ 7

㉒
15
÷ 5

㉓
132
÷ 12

㉔
55
÷ 11

㉕
33
÷ 11

㉖
24
÷ 12

㉗
15
÷ 3

㉘
30
÷ 3

㉙
36
÷ 3

㉚
84
÷ 7

㉛
20
÷ 5

㉜
30
÷ 3

㉝
30
÷ 3

㉞
72
÷ 9

㉟
27
÷ 9

Score		Time		Worksheet 77	Name	

① 108 ÷ 12	② 42 ÷ 7	③ 30 ÷ 10	④ 60 ÷ 10	⑤ 96 ÷ 12	⑥ 36 ÷ 12	⑦ 45 ÷ 9
⑧ 15 ÷ 3	⑨ 15 ÷ 3	⑩ 72 ÷ 9	⑪ 49 ÷ 7	⑫ 30 ÷ 10	⑬ 36 ÷ 9	⑭ 45 ÷ 9
⑮ 10 ÷ 2	⑯ 72 ÷ 12	⑰ 45 ÷ 5	⑱ 132 ÷ 11	⑲ 56 ÷ 8	⑳ 60 ÷ 6	㉑ 56 ÷ 7
㉒ 99 ÷ 9	㉓ 30 ÷ 6	㉔ 15 ÷ 5	㉕ 16 ÷ 8	㉖ 8 ÷ 4	㉗ 14 ÷ 2	㉘ 18 ÷ 3
㉙ 40 ÷ 4	㉚ 48 ÷ 6	㉛ 30 ÷ 10	㉜ 12 ÷ 4	㉝ 110 ÷ 11	㉞ 28 ÷ 7	㉟ 12 ÷ 3

①
$$48 \div 6$$

②
$$36 \div 4$$

③
$$132 \div 12$$

④
$$99 \div 11$$

⑤
$$144 \div 12$$

⑥
$$24 \div 12$$

⑦
$$64 \div 8$$

⑧
$$30 \div 3$$

⑨
$$60 \div 6$$

⑩
$$40 \div 5$$

⑪
$$16 \div 4$$

⑫
$$55 \div 11$$

⑬
$$49 \div 7$$

⑭
$$108 \div 9$$

⑮
$$70 \div 10$$

⑯
$$32 \div 4$$

⑰
$$132 \div 11$$

⑱
$$16 \div 4$$

⑲
$$22 \div 11$$

⑳
$$36 \div 9$$

㉑
$$12 \div 4$$

㉒
$$22 \div 2$$

㉓
$$54 \div 9$$

㉔
$$55 \div 5$$

㉕
$$40 \div 5$$

㉖
$$54 \div 9$$

㉗
$$27 \div 3$$

㉘
$$60 \div 5$$

㉙
$$32 \div 8$$

㉚
$$66 \div 11$$

㉛
$$110 \div 10$$

㉜
$$66 \div 11$$

㉝
$$40 \div 10$$

㉞
$$40 \div 5$$

㉟
$$132 \div 12$$

①
24
÷ 12

②
35
÷ 5

③
24
÷ 12

④
32
÷ 8

⑤
48
÷ 6

⑥
45
÷ 9

⑦
22
÷ 11

⑧
132
÷ 11

⑨
24
÷ 8

⑩
14
÷ 7

⑪
40
÷ 10

⑫
30
÷ 5

⑬
55
÷ 5

⑭
33
÷ 3

⑮
48
÷ 4

⑯
110
÷ 11

⑰
28
÷ 4

⑱
77
÷ 11

⑲
77
÷ 7

⑳
16
÷ 4

㉑
32
÷ 8

㉒
48
÷ 8

㉓
144
÷ 12

㉔
24
÷ 6

㉕
24
÷ 3

㉖
36
÷ 4

㉗
84
÷ 7

㉘
99
÷ 9

㉙
56
÷ 8

㉚
28
÷ 4

㉛
80
÷ 8

㉜
48
÷ 8

㉝
42
÷ 6

㉞
72
÷ 8

㉟
44
÷ 4

①
$$32 \div 8$$

②
$$49 \div 7$$

③
$$35 \div 5$$

④
$$36 \div 6$$

⑤
$$48 \div 6$$

⑥
$$120 \div 12$$

⑦
$$110 \div 10$$

⑧
$$22 \div 11$$

⑨
$$50 \div 10$$

⑩
$$120 \div 10$$

⑪
$$60 \div 6$$

⑫
$$44 \div 4$$

⑬
$$18 \div 2$$

⑭
$$88 \div 8$$

⑮
$$77 \div 7$$

⑯
$$99 \div 11$$

⑰
$$60 \div 5$$

⑱
$$132 \div 12$$

⑲
$$90 \div 9$$

⑳
$$24 \div 6$$

㉑
$$22 \div 2$$

㉒
$$77 \div 7$$

㉓
$$72 \div 12$$

㉔
$$121 \div 11$$

㉕
$$80 \div 8$$

㉖
$$20 \div 4$$

㉗
$$44 \div 11$$

㉘
$$33 \div 3$$

㉙
$$18 \div 3$$

㉚
$$4 \div 2$$

㉛
$$81 \div 9$$

㉜
$$84 \div 12$$

㉝
$$90 \div 10$$

㉞
$$36 \div 12$$

㉟
$$20 \div 5$$

①
60
÷ 12

②
88
÷ 11

③
72
÷ 8

④
21
÷ 7

⑤
48
÷ 4

⑥
36
÷ 9

⑦
72
÷ 9

⑧
48
÷ 12

⑨
12
÷ 4

⑩
63
÷ 9

⑪
12
÷ 3

⑫
15
÷ 5

⑬
30
÷ 10

⑭
30
÷ 6

⑮
60
÷ 10

⑯
88
÷ 11

⑰
48
÷ 6

⑱
18
÷ 3

⑲
12
÷ 2

⑳
30
÷ 5

㉑
45
÷ 5

㉒
20
÷ 10

㉓
42
÷ 7

㉔
18
÷ 3

㉕
45
÷ 9

㉖
18
÷ 9

㉗
40
÷ 4

㉘
44
÷ 4

㉙
33
÷ 3

㉚
20
÷ 10

㉛
84
÷ 12

㉜
63
÷ 7

㉝
108
÷ 12

㉞
48
÷ 8

㉟
90
÷ 10

① 10 ÷ 5

② 18 ÷ 2

③ 66 ÷ 6

④ 15 ÷ 3

⑤ 30 ÷ 5

⑥ 66 ÷ 6

⑦ 48 ÷ 12

⑧ 60 ÷ 12

⑨ 16 ÷ 4

⑩ 32 ÷ 8

⑪ 55 ÷ 5

⑫ 30 ÷ 10

⑬ 80 ÷ 10

⑭ 14 ÷ 2

⑮ 84 ÷ 12

⑯ 15 ÷ 5

⑰ 16 ÷ 2

⑱ 18 ÷ 2

⑲ 15 ÷ 5

⑳ 35 ÷ 5

㉑ 90 ÷ 9

㉒ 16 ÷ 8

㉓ 42 ÷ 7

㉔ 36 ÷ 9

㉕ 120 ÷ 10

㉖ 55 ÷ 5

㉗ 90 ÷ 9

㉘ 84 ÷ 7

㉙ 64 ÷ 8

㉚ 120 ÷ 10

㉛ 16 ÷ 4

㉜ 96 ÷ 8

㉝ 63 ÷ 9

㉞ 24 ÷ 6

㉟ 36 ÷ 12

①
　　18
÷　6

②
　　66
÷　6

③
　120
÷　10

④
　　16
÷　2

⑤
　　72
÷　9

⑥
　　36
÷　3

⑦
　　84
÷　7

⑧
　　40
÷　10

⑨
　　28
÷　7

⑩
　　20
÷　5

⑪
　　63
÷　7

⑫
　　9
÷　3

⑬
　　30
÷　6

⑭
　　33
÷　11

⑮
　　35
÷　7

⑯
　　24
÷　3

⑰
　　32
÷　8

⑱
　　24
÷　8

⑲
　　96
÷　12

⑳
　　48
÷　12

㉑
　　28
÷　4

㉒
　　10
÷　5

㉓
　　12
÷　3

㉔
　　32
÷　4

㉕
　　40
÷　5

㉖
　　8
÷　4

㉗
　　77
÷　7

㉘
　　56
÷　8

㉙
　　44
÷　4

㉚
　　84
÷　12

㉛
　　6
÷　2

㉜
　120
÷　10

㉝
　　40
÷　10

㉞
　　28
÷　4

㉟
　　72
÷　8

①
$$14 \div 2$$

②
$$50 \div 10$$

③
$$30 \div 3$$

④
$$30 \div 5$$

⑤
$$100 \div 10$$

⑥
$$48 \div 12$$

⑦
$$32 \div 4$$

⑧
$$54 \div 9$$

⑨
$$36 \div 6$$

⑩
$$9 \div 3$$

⑪
$$120 \div 10$$

⑫
$$80 \div 8$$

⑬
$$16 \div 8$$

⑭
$$60 \div 5$$

⑮
$$12 \div 3$$

⑯
$$72 \div 12$$

⑰
$$44 \div 11$$

⑱
$$32 \div 4$$

⑲
$$14 \div 7$$

⑳
$$8 \div 2$$

㉑
$$32 \div 8$$

㉒
$$40 \div 8$$

㉓
$$12 \div 4$$

㉔
$$121 \div 11$$

㉕
$$45 \div 9$$

㉖
$$24 \div 8$$

㉗
$$42 \div 7$$

㉘
$$40 \div 4$$

㉙
$$15 \div 3$$

㉚
$$30 \div 3$$

㉛
$$6 \div 2$$

㉜
$$54 \div 9$$

㉝
$$10 \div 2$$

㉞
$$32 \div 4$$

㉟
$$16 \div 4$$

①
24
÷ 12

②
96
÷ 12

③
27
÷ 9

④
33
÷ 3

⑤
100
÷ 10

⑥
18
÷ 2

⑦
42
÷ 7

⑧
90
÷ 10

⑨
63
÷ 7

⑩
144
÷ 12

⑪
12
÷ 2

⑫
70
÷ 10

⑬
40
÷ 4

⑭
30
÷ 10

⑮
55
÷ 5

⑯
30
÷ 10

⑰
100
÷ 10

⑱
32
÷ 8

⑲
15
÷ 3

⑳
30
÷ 6

㉑
10
÷ 2

㉒
48
÷ 4

㉓
120
÷ 10

㉔
8
÷ 2

㉕
63
÷ 9

㉖
64
÷ 8

㉗
30
÷ 10

㉘
40
÷ 5

㉙
108
÷ 12

㉚
36
÷ 9

㉛
33
÷ 3

㉜
14
÷ 7

㉝
45
÷ 5

㉞
30
÷ 10

㉟
48
÷ 4

① 60 ÷ 10

② 60 ÷ 10

③ 55 ÷ 11

④ 20 ÷ 10

⑤ 4 ÷ 2

⑥ 14 ÷ 7

⑦ 108 ÷ 12

⑧ 22 ÷ 11

⑨ 33 ÷ 11

⑩ 30 ÷ 6

⑪ 72 ÷ 9

⑫ 22 ÷ 2

⑬ 88 ÷ 8

⑭ 96 ÷ 8

⑮ 88 ÷ 11

⑯ 42 ÷ 6

⑰ 70 ÷ 7

⑱ 84 ÷ 7

⑲ 48 ÷ 12

⑳ 27 ÷ 3

㉑ 72 ÷ 9

㉒ 55 ÷ 11

㉓ 14 ÷ 2

㉔ 18 ÷ 6

㉕ 36 ÷ 6

㉖ 24 ÷ 8

㉗ 72 ÷ 6

㉘ 44 ÷ 11

㉙ 72 ÷ 6

㉚ 33 ÷ 3

㉛ 96 ÷ 12

㉜ 80 ÷ 8

㉝ 18 ÷ 6

㉞ 60 ÷ 12

㉟ 60 ÷ 10

① 45 ÷ 5

② 99 ÷ 11

③ 20 ÷ 10

④ 72 ÷ 12

⑤ 110 ÷ 11

⑥ 24 ÷ 6

⑦ 22 ÷ 11

⑧ 20 ÷ 4

⑨ 132 ÷ 11

⑩ 14 ÷ 2

⑪ 60 ÷ 12

⑫ 32 ÷ 4

⑬ 15 ÷ 3

⑭ 32 ÷ 4

⑮ 18 ÷ 6

⑯ 48 ÷ 12

⑰ 36 ÷ 6

⑱ 88 ÷ 11

⑲ 27 ÷ 3

⑳ 36 ÷ 3

㉑ 63 ÷ 7

㉒ 12 ÷ 4

㉓ 49 ÷ 7

㉔ 12 ÷ 2

㉕ 12 ÷ 2

㉖ 72 ÷ 8

㉗ 84 ÷ 12

㉘ 70 ÷ 7

㉙ 16 ÷ 2

㉚ 70 ÷ 7

㉛ 48 ÷ 8

㉜ 25 ÷ 5

㉝ 24 ÷ 6

㉞ 56 ÷ 8

㉟ 40 ÷ 10

①
$$35 \div 5$$

②
$$99 \div 9$$

③
$$40 \div 8$$

④
$$35 \div 5$$

⑤
$$64 \div 8$$

⑥
$$9 \div 3$$

⑦
$$90 \div 9$$

⑧
$$100 \div 10$$

⑨
$$99 \div 11$$

⑩
$$80 \div 8$$

⑪
$$32 \div 4$$

⑫
$$108 \div 9$$

⑬
$$20 \div 10$$

⑭
$$6 \div 3$$

⑮
$$15 \div 5$$

⑯
$$30 \div 5$$

⑰
$$72 \div 9$$

⑱
$$50 \div 5$$

⑲
$$70 \div 10$$

⑳
$$56 \div 7$$

㉑
$$16 \div 8$$

㉒
$$56 \div 7$$

㉓
$$4 \div 2$$

㉔
$$10 \div 5$$

㉕
$$22 \div 11$$

㉖
$$12 \div 3$$

㉗
$$42 \div 6$$

㉘
$$77 \div 7$$

㉙
$$24 \div 3$$

㉚
$$80 \div 8$$

㉛
$$81 \div 9$$

㉜
$$110 \div 10$$

㉝
$$18 \div 2$$

㉞
$$42 \div 7$$

㉟
$$44 \div 11$$

① 27 ÷ 9

② 28 ÷ 7

③ 28 ÷ 4

④ 21 ÷ 7

⑤ 25 ÷ 5

⑥ 33 ÷ 11

⑦ 44 ÷ 11

⑧ 36 ÷ 12

⑨ 22 ÷ 2

⑩ 80 ÷ 8

⑪ 42 ÷ 6

⑫ 10 ÷ 5

⑬ 108 ÷ 12

⑭ 120 ÷ 12

⑮ 96 ÷ 12

⑯ 22 ÷ 11

⑰ 18 ÷ 2

⑱ 20 ÷ 4

⑲ 12 ÷ 4

⑳ 36 ÷ 4

㉑ 56 ÷ 7

㉒ 18 ÷ 2

㉓ 48 ÷ 12

㉔ 40 ÷ 5

㉕ 110 ÷ 10

㉖ 28 ÷ 4

㉗ 48 ÷ 8

㉘ 10 ÷ 2

㉙ 90 ÷ 10

㉚ 99 ÷ 9

㉛ 132 ÷ 11

㉜ 72 ÷ 6

㉝ 72 ÷ 8

㉞ 96 ÷ 8

㉟ 56 ÷ 7

①
20
÷ 4

②
44
÷ 11

③
96
÷ 8

④
30
÷ 6

⑤
15
÷ 3

⑥
70
÷ 10

⑦
63
÷ 9

⑧
15
÷ 3

⑨
72
÷ 6

⑩
66
÷ 6

⑪
35
÷ 7

⑫
50
÷ 5

⑬
55
÷ 5

⑭
60
÷ 6

⑮
16
÷ 4

⑯
70
÷ 7

⑰
56
÷ 7

⑱
72
÷ 9

⑲
84
÷ 7

⑳
15
÷ 5

㉑
90
÷ 10

㉒
40
÷ 5

㉓
4
÷ 2

㉔
60
÷ 6

㉕
8
÷ 4

㉖
22
÷ 2

㉗
42
÷ 6

㉘
72
÷ 6

㉙
40
÷ 4

㉚
40
÷ 10

㉛
50
÷ 10

㉜
14
÷ 7

㉝
60
÷ 12

㉞
20
÷ 5

㉟
60
÷ 10

①
$$30 \div 10$$

②
$$33 \div 11$$

③
$$70 \div 7$$

④
$$21 \div 3$$

⑤
$$24 \div 2$$

⑥
$$14 \div 7$$

⑦
$$36 \div 9$$

⑧
$$120 \div 10$$

⑨
$$121 \div 11$$

⑩
$$56 \div 8$$

⑪
$$30 \div 10$$

⑫
$$44 \div 4$$

⑬
$$54 \div 6$$

⑭
$$12 \div 3$$

⑮
$$24 \div 12$$

⑯
$$40 \div 10$$

⑰
$$42 \div 6$$

⑱
$$6 \div 3$$

⑲
$$21 \div 3$$

⑳
$$48 \div 12$$

㉑
$$80 \div 10$$

㉒
$$100 \div 10$$

㉓
$$12 \div 2$$

㉔
$$132 \div 11$$

㉕
$$25 \div 5$$

㉖
$$56 \div 7$$

㉗
$$6 \div 2$$

㉘
$$28 \div 7$$

㉙
$$36 \div 3$$

㉚
$$28 \div 4$$

㉛
$$132 \div 12$$

㉜
$$10 \div 5$$

㉝
$$45 \div 9$$

㉞
$$96 \div 8$$

㉟
$$45 \div 5$$

①
50
÷ 5

②
110
÷ 10

③
84
÷ 12

④
24
÷ 12

⑤
90
÷ 9

⑥
54
÷ 9

⑦
14
÷ 2

⑧
81
÷ 9

⑨
99
÷ 11

⑩
28
÷ 4

⑪
32
÷ 4

⑫
16
÷ 4

⑬
84
÷ 7

⑭
42
÷ 6

⑮
18
÷ 6

⑯
100
÷ 10

⑰
12
÷ 4

⑱
108
÷ 9

⑲
60
÷ 10

⑳
24
÷ 4

㉑
25
÷ 5

㉒
110
÷ 11

㉓
24
÷ 2

㉔
50
÷ 10

㉕
60
÷ 6

㉖
16
÷ 2

㉗
60
÷ 6

㉘
42
÷ 7

㉙
10
÷ 5

㉚
27
÷ 9

㉛
16
÷ 2

㉜
96
÷ 12

㉝
42
÷ 7

㉞
28
÷ 4

㉟
72
÷ 8

① 24 ÷ 8

② 40 ÷ 4

③ 18 ÷ 9

④ 24 ÷ 6

⑤ 100 ÷ 10

⑥ 90 ÷ 9

⑦ 108 ÷ 12

⑧ 6 ÷ 2

⑨ 12 ÷ 4

⑩ 27 ÷ 3

⑪ 88 ÷ 11

⑫ 99 ÷ 11

⑬ 36 ÷ 9

⑭ 48 ÷ 12

⑮ 18 ÷ 3

⑯ 27 ÷ 9

⑰ 49 ÷ 7

⑱ 6 ÷ 3

⑲ 84 ÷ 12

⑳ 6 ÷ 3

㉑ 50 ÷ 10

㉒ 14 ÷ 2

㉓ 77 ÷ 11

㉔ 44 ÷ 4

㉕ 24 ÷ 3

㉖ 72 ÷ 6

㉗ 72 ÷ 12

㉘ 96 ÷ 12

㉙ 27 ÷ 9

㉚ 15 ÷ 5

㉛ 22 ÷ 2

㉜ 63 ÷ 9

㉝ 14 ÷ 7

㉞ 10 ÷ 2

㉟ 70 ÷ 10

①
14
÷ 2

②
30
÷ 6

③
24
÷ 8

④
72
÷ 8

⑤
72
÷ 12

⑥
30
÷ 6

⑦
60
÷ 10

⑧
30
÷ 5

⑨
66
÷ 11

⑩
22
÷ 11

⑪
81
÷ 9

⑫
72
÷ 9

⑬
84
÷ 12

⑭
64
÷ 8

⑮
120
÷ 12

⑯
90
÷ 9

⑰
60
÷ 6

⑱
48
÷ 12

⑲
24
÷ 4

⑳
14
÷ 7

㉑
80
÷ 8

㉒
25
÷ 5

㉓
24
÷ 6

㉔
99
÷ 11

㉕
36
÷ 4

㉖
36
÷ 4

㉗
42
÷ 7

㉘
40
÷ 5

㉙
45
÷ 9

㉚
21
÷ 7

㉛
27
÷ 9

㉜
27
÷ 9

㉝
36
÷ 4

㉞
42
÷ 6

㉟
18
÷ 9

①
63
÷ 7

②
15
÷ 5

③
18
÷ 2

④
63
÷ 7

⑤
72
÷ 6

⑥
88
÷ 11

⑦
27
÷ 9

⑧
18
÷ 9

⑨
32
÷ 4

⑩
33
÷ 11

⑪
16
÷ 8

⑫
4
÷ 2

⑬
15
÷ 5

⑭
60
÷ 10

⑮
24
÷ 8

⑯
63
÷ 7

⑰
63
÷ 9

⑱
6
÷ 3

⑲
72
÷ 9

⑳
108
÷ 12

㉑
56
÷ 8

㉒
12
÷ 4

㉓
120
÷ 12

㉔
96
÷ 8

㉕
40
÷ 8

㉖
30
÷ 10

㉗
12
÷ 2

㉘
33
÷ 11

㉙
110
÷ 10

㉚
32
÷ 4

㉛
45
÷ 9

㉜
4
÷ 2

㉝
63
÷ 7

㉞
120
÷ 12

㉟
66
÷ 6

①
$$90 \div 10$$

②
$$30 \div 3$$

③
$$96 \div 8$$

④
$$4 \div 2$$

⑤
$$48 \div 8$$

⑥
$$33 \div 11$$

⑦
$$88 \div 11$$

⑧
$$32 \div 8$$

⑨
$$110 \div 11$$

⑩
$$25 \div 5$$

⑪
$$35 \div 5$$

⑫
$$55 \div 11$$

⑬
$$42 \div 6$$

⑭
$$49 \div 7$$

⑮
$$84 \div 7$$

⑯
$$132 \div 12$$

⑰
$$120 \div 12$$

⑱
$$8 \div 2$$

⑲
$$132 \div 11$$

⑳
$$36 \div 9$$

㉑
$$55 \div 11$$

㉒
$$96 \div 12$$

㉓
$$32 \div 4$$

㉔
$$25 \div 5$$

㉕
$$30 \div 3$$

㉖
$$64 \div 8$$

㉗
$$20 \div 10$$

㉘
$$18 \div 3$$

㉙
$$84 \div 12$$

㉚
$$90 \div 10$$

㉛
$$110 \div 10$$

㉜
$$24 \div 2$$

㉝
$$24 \div 2$$

㉞
$$36 \div 4$$

㉟
$$56 \div 7$$

① 144 ÷ 12

② 88 ÷ 8

③ 12 ÷ 6

④ 10 ÷ 5

⑤ 60 ÷ 10

⑥ 9 ÷ 3

⑦ 16 ÷ 2

⑧ 66 ÷ 6

⑨ 50 ÷ 10

⑩ 33 ÷ 3

⑪ 27 ÷ 9

⑫ 48 ÷ 8

⑬ 80 ÷ 8

⑭ 48 ÷ 4

⑮ 48 ÷ 12

⑯ 18 ÷ 9

⑰ 20 ÷ 4

⑱ 72 ÷ 6

⑲ 12 ÷ 4

⑳ 20 ÷ 2

㉑ 24 ÷ 12

㉒ 60 ÷ 10

㉓ 40 ÷ 4

㉔ 63 ÷ 7

㉕ 72 ÷ 8

㉖ 28 ÷ 4

㉗ 18 ÷ 6

㉘ 27 ÷ 3

㉙ 12 ÷ 2

㉚ 42 ÷ 7

㉛ 4 ÷ 2

㉜ 55 ÷ 5

㉝ 45 ÷ 9

㉞ 144 ÷ 12

㉟ 12 ÷ 4

① 15 ÷ 5

② 16 ÷ 2

③ 20 ÷ 10

④ 80 ÷ 10

⑤ 4 ÷ 2

⑥ 60 ÷ 6

⑦ 72 ÷ 6

⑧ 28 ÷ 7

⑨ 56 ÷ 7

⑩ 40 ÷ 8

⑪ 20 ÷ 10

⑫ 63 ÷ 7

⑬ 12 ÷ 3

⑭ 77 ÷ 7

⑮ 20 ÷ 4

⑯ 10 ÷ 2

⑰ 15 ÷ 3

⑱ 35 ÷ 5

⑲ 88 ÷ 8

⑳ 16 ÷ 4

㉑ 121 ÷ 11

㉒ 9 ÷ 3

㉓ 84 ÷ 12

㉔ 63 ÷ 9

㉕ 96 ÷ 12

㉖ 15 ÷ 3

㉗ 60 ÷ 5

㉘ 18 ÷ 6

㉙ 20 ÷ 2

㉚ 28 ÷ 7

㉛ 56 ÷ 8

㉜ 10 ÷ 5

㉝ 108 ÷ 9

㉞ 12 ÷ 6

㉟ 54 ÷ 9

①
6
÷ 2

②
70
÷ 10

③
12
÷ 3

④
24
÷ 4

⑤
24
÷ 6

⑥
16
÷ 2

⑦
24
÷ 4

⑧
33
÷ 11

⑨
12
÷ 2

⑩
144
÷ 12

⑪
32
÷ 8

⑫
77
÷ 7

⑬
42
÷ 7

⑭
8
÷ 2

⑮
81
÷ 9

⑯
120
÷ 12

⑰
45
÷ 5

⑱
55
÷ 11

⑲
48
÷ 12

⑳
20
÷ 2

㉑
27
÷ 3

㉒
20
÷ 10

㉓
48
÷ 12

㉔
42
÷ 7

㉕
63
÷ 7

㉖
60
÷ 12

㉗
144
÷ 12

㉘
56
÷ 8

㉙
81
÷ 9

㉚
12
÷ 6

㉛
54
÷ 6

㉜
88
÷ 8

㉝
15
÷ 3

㉞
8
÷ 4

㉟
88
÷ 11

①
14
÷ 7

②
6
÷ 3

③
40
÷ 4

④
88
÷ 8

⑤
42
÷ 6

⑥
49
÷ 7

⑦
72
÷ 12

⑧
35
÷ 5

⑨
12
÷ 2

⑩
108
÷ 9

⑪
30
÷ 3

⑫
35
÷ 7

⑬
48
÷ 8

⑭
99
÷ 9

⑮
63
÷ 9

⑯
60
÷ 10

⑰
40
÷ 8

⑱
21
÷ 7

⑲
20
÷ 5

⑳
15
÷ 3

㉑
16
÷ 8

㉒
72
÷ 9

㉓
81
÷ 9

㉔
15
÷ 3

㉕
108
÷ 12

㉖
25
÷ 5

㉗
42
÷ 6

㉘
30
÷ 3

㉙
45
÷ 5

㉚
18
÷ 2

㉛
72
÷ 9

㉜
48
÷ 4

㉝
27
÷ 3

㉞
77
÷ 11

㉟
96
÷ 8

ANSWERS

Worksheet 1

①	8	②	2	③	8	④	4	⑤	6	⑥	8	⑦	7
⑧	1	⑨	7	⑩	1	⑪	4	⑫	6	⑬	1	⑭	9
⑮	10	⑯	7	⑰	8	⑱	3	⑲	0	⑳	0	㉑	10
㉒	0	㉓	9	㉔	4	㉕	9	㉖	8	㉗	1	㉘	1
㉙	8	㉚	6	㉛	0	㉜	6	㉝	8	㉞	10	㉟	1

Worksheet 2

①	7	②	4	③	0	④	7	⑤	2	⑥	5	⑦	1
⑧	2	⑨	9	⑩	7	⑪	3	⑫	2	⑬	6	⑭	10
⑮	9	⑯	1	⑰	8	⑱	6	⑲	1	⑳	0	㉑	3
㉒	7	㉓	10	㉔	1	㉕	7	㉖	8	㉗	2	㉘	0
㉙	0	㉚	10	㉛	1	㉜	1	㉝	6	㉞	0	㉟	0

Worksheet 3

①	8	②	7	③	6	④	8	⑤	5	⑥	10	⑦	4
⑧	0	⑨	1	⑩	1	⑪	8	⑫	4	⑬	2	⑭	7
⑮	8	⑯	3	⑰	4	⑱	10	⑲	6	⑳	6	㉑	1
㉒	4	㉓	7	㉔	2	㉕	8	㉖	0	㉗	8	㉘	2
㉙	9	㉚	1	㉛	0	㉜	9	㉝	0	㉞	9	㉟	4

Worksheet 4

①	9	②	6	③	9	④	1	⑤	0	⑥	9	⑦	0
⑧	5	⑨	9	⑩	1	⑪	3	⑫	6	⑬	8	⑭	9
⑮	4	⑯	4	⑰	9	⑱	1	⑲	8	⑳	4	㉑	8
㉒	3	㉓	8	㉔	3	㉕	3	㉖	4	㉗	5	㉘	0
㉙	8	㉚	6	㉛	2	㉜	9	㉝	3	㉞	8	㉟	6

Worksheet 5

①	5	②	4	③	5	④	8	⑤	3	⑥	4	⑦	1
⑧	5	⑨	6	⑩	4	⑪	6	⑫	10	⑬	1	⑭	8
⑮	5	⑯	10	⑰	1	⑱	7	⑲	1	⑳	6	㉑	5
㉒	6	㉓	9	㉔	6	㉕	3	㉖	9	㉗	8	㉘	6
㉙	8	㉚	5	㉛	5	㉜	4	㉝	1	㉞	10	㉟	2

Worksheet 6

①	10	②	6	③	6	④	7	⑤	5	⑥	0	⑦	7
⑧	8	⑨	7	⑩	6	⑪	4	⑫	2	⑬	10	⑭	2
⑮	2	⑯	9	⑰	10	⑱	10	⑲	6	⑳	5	㉑	2
㉒	7	㉓	0	㉔	5	㉕	8	㉖	1	㉗	5	㉘	4
㉙	8	㉚	10	㉛	6	㉜	9	㉝	3	㉞	4	㉟	0

Worksheet 7

①	3	②	7	③	0	④	10	⑤	3	⑥	9	⑦	5
⑧	6	⑨	2	⑩	2	⑪	7	⑫	2	⑬	0	⑭	1
⑮	9	⑯	4	⑰	6	⑱	4	⑲	9	⑳	10	㉑	3
㉒	5	㉓	3	㉔	9	㉕	10	㉖	3	㉗	9	㉘	6
㉙	2	㉚	8	㉛	5	㉜	7	㉝	2	㉞	10	㉟	2

Worksheet 8

①	10	②	7	③	2	④	9	⑤	3	⑥	4	⑦	4
⑧	3	⑨	9	⑩	2	⑪	3	⑫	9	⑬	7	⑭	2
⑮	2	⑯	7	⑰	10	⑱	10	⑲	0	⑳	2	㉑	10
㉒	10	㉓	9	㉔	7	㉕	0	㉖	5	㉗	6	㉘	5
㉙	7	㉚	9	㉛	10	㉜	9	㉝	10	㉞	5	㉟	2

Worksheet 9

①	3	②	5	③	6	④	8	⑤	3	⑥	5	⑦	9
⑧	7	⑨	10	⑩	4	⑪	1	⑫	8	⑬	2	⑭	10
⑮	9	⑯	3	⑰	6	⑱	0	⑲	4	⑳	0	㉑	7
㉒	9	㉓	5	㉔	6	㉕	2	㉖	9	㉗	3	㉘	10
㉙	3	㉚	6	㉛	0	㉜	6	㉝	7	㉞	6	㉟	9

Worksheet 10

① 5	② 8	③ 0	④ 0	⑤ 6	⑥ 2	⑦ 10	
⑧ 1	⑨ 1	⑩ 4	⑪ 10	⑫ 10	⑬ 8	⑭ 10	
⑮ 7	⑯ 8	⑰ 2	⑱ 0	⑲ 3	⑳ 1	㉑ 6	
㉒ 7	㉓ 6	㉔ 9	㉕ 10	㉖ 1	㉗ 3	㉘ 6	
㉙ 2	㉚ 10	㉛ 7	㉜ 2	㉝ 2	㉞ 10	㉟ 8	

Worksheet 11

① 9	② 8	③ 2	④ 0	⑤ 1	⑥ 1	⑦ 0	
⑧ 2	⑨ 1	⑩ 10	⑪ 10	⑫ 5	⑬ 6	⑭ 6	
⑮ 4	⑯ 0	⑰ 0	⑱ 3	⑲ 10	⑳ 4	㉑ 3	
㉒ 6	㉓ 5	㉔ 2	㉕ 7	㉖ 3	㉗ 3	㉘ 2	
㉙ 3	㉚ 9	㉛ 4	㉜ 5	㉝ 0	㉞ 8	㉟ 1	

Worksheet 12

① 2	② 9	③ 7	④ 9	⑤ 3	⑥ 0	⑦ 8	
⑧ 5	⑨ 0	⑩ 7	⑪ 7	⑫ 2	⑬ 1	⑭ 3	
⑮ 7	⑯ 4	⑰ 7	⑱ 6	⑲ 7	⑳ 8	㉑ 4	
㉒ 0	㉓ 4	㉔ 7	㉕ 1	㉖ 4	㉗ 2	㉘ 9	
㉙ 8	㉚ 5	㉛ 7	㉜ 5	㉝ 4	㉞ 3	㉟ 9	

Worksheet 13

① 10	② 5	③ 4	④ 1	⑤ 3	⑥ 8	⑦ 5	
⑧ 0	⑨ 4	⑩ 4	⑪ 2	⑫ 6	⑬ 5	⑭ 3	
⑮ 3	⑯ 7	⑰ 6	⑱ 0	⑲ 10	⑳ 2	㉑ 4	
㉒ 8	㉓ 3	㉔ 7	㉕ 0	㉖ 3	㉗ 7	㉘ 8	
㉙ 2	㉚ 3	㉛ 1	㉜ 0	㉝ 6	㉞ 4	㉟ 5	

Worksheet 14

① 7	② 1	③ 1	④ 4	⑤ 7	⑥ 8	⑦ 6	
⑧ 9	⑨ 1	⑩ 10	⑪ 1	⑫ 9	⑬ 5	⑭ 9	
⑮ 2	⑯ 9	⑰ 0	⑱ 10	⑲ 5	⑳ 2	㉑ 1	
㉒ 4	㉓ 10	㉔ 6	㉕ 8	㉖ 10	㉗ 6	㉘ 1	
㉙ 0	㉚ 3	㉛ 9	㉜ 3	㉝ 6	㉞ 6	㉟ 0	

Worksheet 15

① 2	② 3	③ 8	④ 6	⑤ 10	⑥ 7	⑦ 2
⑧ 6	⑨ 3	⑩ 6	⑪ 5	⑫ 0	⑬ 2	⑭ 8
⑮ 5	⑯ 3	⑰ 4	⑱ 3	⑲ 10	⑳ 4	㉑ 1
㉒ 10	㉓ 4	㉔ 0	㉕ 2	㉖ 7	㉗ 7	㉘ 8
㉙ 5	㉚ 8	㉛ 10	㉜ 5	㉝ 8	㉞ 7	㉟ 4

Worksheet 16

① 10	② 7	③ 3	④ 10	⑤ 9	⑥ 1	⑦ 7
⑧ 8	⑨ 9	⑩ 7	⑪ 2	⑫ 7	⑬ 10	⑭ 4
⑮ 9	⑯ 2	⑰ 1	⑱ 5	⑲ 10	⑳ 6	㉑ 8
㉒ 10	㉓ 7	㉔ 9	㉕ 6	㉖ 3	㉗ 7	㉘ 10
㉙ 1	㉚ 5	㉛ 6	㉜ 4	㉝ 4	㉞ 6	㉟ 10

Worksheet 17

① 9	② 2	③ 1	④ 4	⑤ 10	⑥ 6	⑦ 10
⑧ 6	⑨ 8	⑩ 4	⑪ 5	⑫ 2	⑬ 4	⑭ 2
⑮ 4	⑯ 4	⑰ 0	⑱ 0	⑲ 9	⑳ 10	㉑ 8
㉒ 7	㉓ 1	㉔ 1	㉕ 9	㉖ 10	㉗ 2	㉘ 3
㉙ 1	㉚ 0	㉛ 8	㉜ 2	㉝ 6	㉞ 3	㉟ 4

Worksheet 18

① 4	② 4	③ 4	④ 3	⑤ 4	⑥ 9	⑦ 3
⑧ 9	⑨ 3	⑩ 1	⑪ 6	⑫ 2	⑬ 5	⑭ 5
⑮ 0	⑯ 3	⑰ 0	⑱ 4	⑲ 5	⑳ 2	㉑ 6
㉒ 2	㉓ 7	㉔ 10	㉕ 6	㉖ 3	㉗ 6	㉘ 5
㉙ 2	㉚ 7	㉛ 2	㉜ 4	㉝ 10	㉞ 6	㉟ 3

Worksheet 19

① 6	② 5	③ 5	④ 7	⑤ 6	⑥ 7	⑦ 3
⑧ 0	⑨ 0	⑩ 0	⑪ 0	⑫ 2	⑬ 1	⑭ 9
⑮ 10	⑯ 9	⑰ 6	⑱ 10	⑲ 10	⑳ 0	㉑ 5
㉒ 3	㉓ 4	㉔ 3	㉕ 4	㉖ 0	㉗ 8	㉘ 2
㉙ 2	㉚ 2	㉛ 0	㉜ 0	㉝ 1	㉞ 8	㉟ 1

Worksheet 20

①	3	②	6	③	5	④	1	⑤	7	⑥	1	⑦	9
⑧	8	⑨	5	⑩	7	⑪	3	⑫	4	⑬	1	⑭	0
⑮	2	⑯	10	⑰	8	⑱	4	⑲	0	⑳	1	㉑	10
㉒	2	㉓	8	㉔	2	㉕	1	㉖	10	㉗	3	㉘	6
㉙	3	㉚	10	㉛	5	㉜	1	㉝	5	㉞	10	㉟	5

Worksheet 21

①	1	②	7	③	4	④	6	⑤	7	⑥	6	⑦	0
⑧	5	⑨	10	⑩	9	⑪	7	⑫	8	⑬	5	⑭	8
⑮	10	⑯	5	⑰	4	⑱	0	⑲	10	⑳	10	㉑	6
㉒	7	㉓	4	㉔	2	㉕	5	㉖	3	㉗	9	㉘	6
㉙	5	㉚	0	㉛	3	㉜	2	㉝	0	㉞	8	㉟	3

Worksheet 22

①	1	②	8	③	6	④	5	⑤	2	⑥	6	⑦	8
⑧	10	⑨	5	⑩	3	⑪	6	⑫	5	⑬	8	⑭	10
⑮	6	⑯	1	⑰	7	⑱	1	⑲	8	⑳	9	㉑	4
㉒	7	㉓	2	㉔	3	㉕	3	㉖	6	㉗	5	㉘	8
㉙	7	㉚	2	㉛	3	㉜	3	㉝	8	㉞	4	㉟	7

Worksheet 23

①	5	②	0	③	3	④	5	⑤	10	⑥	0	⑦	6
⑧	7	⑨	3	⑩	3	⑪	7	⑫	1	⑬	9	⑭	8
⑮	3	⑯	0	⑰	0	⑱	3	⑲	7	⑳	5	㉑	5
㉒	2	㉓	6	㉔	7	㉕	7	㉖	9	㉗	7	㉘	6
㉙	6	㉚	0	㉛	8	㉜	1	㉝	7	㉞	3	㉟	1

Worksheet 24

①	8	②	9	③	1	④	0	⑤	7	⑥	0	⑦	0
⑧	6	⑨	5	⑩	7	⑪	3	⑫	8	⑬	4	⑭	6
⑮	2	⑯	9	⑰	6	⑱	9	⑲	2	⑳	1	㉑	8
㉒	9	㉓	6	㉔	2	㉕	2	㉖	0	㉗	5	㉘	0
㉙	4	㉚	4	㉛	4	㉜	6	㉝	2	㉞	4	㉟	1

Worksheet 25

① 8	② 1	③ 2	④ 4	⑤ 9	⑥ 10	⑦ 8
⑧ 10	⑨ 8	⑩ 8	⑪ 4	⑫ 3	⑬ 3	⑭ 4
⑮ 0	⑯ 6	⑰ 2	⑱ 3	⑲ 5	⑳ 9	㉑ 8
㉒ 6	㉓ 6	㉔ 10	㉕ 8	㉖ 8	㉗ 8	㉘ 6
㉙ 10	㉚ 4	㉛ 6	㉜ 7	㉝ 6	㉞ 2	㉟ 2

Worksheet 26

① 6	② 8	③ 10	④ 9	⑤ 4	⑥ 10	⑦ 9
⑧ 0	⑨ 3	⑩ 8	⑪ 2	⑫ 2	⑬ 10	⑭ 0
⑮ 4	⑯ 7	⑰ 5	⑱ 10	⑲ 6	⑳ 2	㉑ 2
㉒ 10	㉓ 3	㉔ 5	㉕ 10	㉖ 7	㉗ 0	㉘ 7
㉙ 9	㉚ 3	㉛ 8	㉜ 3	㉝ 1	㉞ 10	㉟ 4

Worksheet 27

① 5	② 2	③ 6	④ 4	⑤ 6	⑥ 3	⑦ 2
⑧ 3	⑨ 6	⑩ 3	⑪ 0	⑫ 0	⑬ 6	⑭ 4
⑮ 2	⑯ 4	⑰ 5	⑱ 10	⑲ 8	⑳ 0	㉑ 4
㉒ 8	㉓ 5	㉔ 4	㉕ 10	㉖ 9	㉗ 3	㉘ 3
㉙ 7	㉚ 6	㉛ 0	㉜ 6	㉝ 0	㉞ 1	㉟ 3

Worksheet 28

① 1	② 10	③ 9	④ 9	⑤ 1	⑥ 3	⑦ 10
⑧ 4	⑨ 6	⑩ 8	⑪ 9	⑫ 3	⑬ 7	⑭ 7
⑮ 10	⑯ 7	⑰ 7	⑱ 6	⑲ 4	⑳ 8	㉑ 2
㉒ 7	㉓ 10	㉔ 3	㉕ 9	㉖ 1	㉗ 3	㉘ 3
㉙ 4	㉚ 6	㉛ 0	㉜ 10	㉝ 2	㉞ 7	㉟ 6

Worksheet 29

① 9	② 2	③ 8	④ 5	⑤ 5	⑥ 4	⑦ 3
⑧ 3	⑨ 5	⑩ 9	⑪ 4	⑫ 10	⑬ 9	⑭ 6
⑮ 6	⑯ 2	⑰ 8	⑱ 5	⑲ 8	⑳ 1	㉑ 10
㉒ 3	㉓ 5	㉔ 9	㉕ 5	㉖ 8	㉗ 7	㉘ 9
㉙ 0	㉚ 10	㉛ 4	㉜ 7	㉝ 7	㉞ 4	㉟ 3

Worksheet 30

①	7	②	8	③	4	④	3	⑤	0	⑥	5	⑦	9
⑧	2	⑨	2	⑩	8	⑪	1	⑫	3	⑬	8	⑭	3
⑮	4	⑯	5	⑰	6	⑱	5	⑲	0	⑳	2	㉑	0
㉒	2	㉓	7	㉔	4	㉕	2	㉖	9	㉗	10	㉘	10
㉙	10	㉚	7	㉛	2	㉜	6	㉝	6	㉞	9	㉟	4

Worksheet 31

①	8	②	4	③	4	④	5	⑤	5	⑥	6	⑦	5
⑧	7	⑨	8	⑩	3	⑪	4	⑫	8	⑬	6	⑭	7
⑮	2	⑯	5	⑰	10	⑱	7	⑲	8	⑳	10	㉑	6
㉒	5	㉓	8	㉔	6	㉕	8	㉖	6	㉗	10	㉘	9
㉙	6	㉚	6	㉛	4	㉜	4	㉝	4	㉞	10	㉟	8

Worksheet 32

①	6	②	2	③	4	④	7	⑤	5	⑥	9	⑦	3
⑧	8	⑨	9	⑩	4	⑪	7	⑫	2	⑬	9	⑭	3
⑮	8	⑯	3	⑰	5	⑱	8	⑲	2	⑳	6	㉑	3
㉒	7	㉓	4	㉔	5	㉕	3	㉖	7	㉗	7	㉘	7
㉙	3	㉚	8	㉛	5	㉜	6	㉝	2	㉞	7	㉟	10

Worksheet 33

①	3	②	10	③	10	④	5	⑤	8	⑥	4	⑦	10
⑧	6	⑨	3	⑩	9	⑪	9	⑫	8	⑬	2	⑭	4
⑮	9	⑯	5	⑰	9	⑱	5	⑲	6	⑳	4	㉑	5
㉒	10	㉓	6	㉔	6	㉕	7	㉖	5	㉗	9	㉘	3
㉙	5	㉚	4	㉛	10	㉜	2	㉝	4	㉞	8	㉟	4

Worksheet 34

①	8	②	6	③	5	④	3	⑤	3	⑥	5	⑦	6
⑧	10	⑨	3	⑩	8	⑪	2	⑫	4	⑬	4	⑭	9
⑮	10	⑯	4	⑰	2	⑱	10	⑲	5	⑳	8	㉑	7
㉒	8	㉓	5	㉔	2	㉕	4	㉖	9	㉗	2	㉘	8
㉙	5	㉚	9	㉛	3	㉜	8	㉝	6	㉞	8	㉟	4

Worksheet 35

①	10	②	2	③	8	④	9	⑤	10	⑥	6	⑦	3
⑧	8	⑨	6	⑩	3	⑪	6	⑫	5	⑬	3	⑭	7
⑮	7	⑯	5	⑰	6	⑱	8	⑲	9	⑳	2	㉑	2
㉒	4	㉓	5	㉔	3	㉕	9	㉖	8	㉗	3	㉘	9
㉙	5	㉚	9	㉛	5	㉜	5	㉝	7	㉞	6	㉟	7

Worksheet 36

①	5	②	7	③	9	④	8	⑤	5	⑥	3	⑦	7
⑧	8	⑨	2	⑩	5	⑪	3	⑫	5	⑬	4	⑭	5
⑮	2	⑯	8	⑰	2	⑱	7	⑲	2	⑳	7	㉑	6
㉒	9	㉓	7	㉔	6	㉕	5	㉖	5	㉗	3	㉘	10
㉙	5	㉚	6	㉛	2	㉜	4	㉝	4	㉞	2	㉟	7

Worksheet 37

①	7	②	8	③	2	④	6	⑤	3	⑥	10	⑦	9
⑧	2	⑨	10	⑩	9	⑪	10	⑫	4	⑬	6	⑭	7
⑮	2	⑯	4	⑰	10	⑱	8	⑲	7	⑳	10	㉑	3
㉒	3	㉓	10	㉔	7	㉕	10	㉖	4	㉗	3	㉘	3
㉙	4	㉚	5	㉛	3	㉜	5	㉝	9	㉞	9	㉟	9

Worksheet 38

①	10	②	10	③	2	④	7	⑤	7	⑥	4	⑦	4
⑧	7	⑨	5	⑩	6	⑪	8	⑫	9	⑬	3	⑭	2
⑮	10	⑯	2	⑰	8	⑱	8	⑲	7	⑳	7	㉑	6
㉒	5	㉓	4	㉔	8	㉕	5	㉖	7	㉗	7	㉘	10
㉙	4	㉚	2	㉛	6	㉜	4	㉝	8	㉞	9	㉟	7

Worksheet 39

①	10	②	4	③	7	④	7	⑤	4	⑥	10	⑦	10
⑧	10	⑨	10	⑩	6	⑪	4	⑫	4	⑬	3	⑭	7
⑮	2	⑯	9	⑰	4	⑱	4	⑲	4	⑳	7	㉑	3
㉒	8	㉓	8	㉔	7	㉕	10	㉖	4	㉗	10	㉘	2
㉙	6	㉚	2	㉛	9	㉜	5	㉝	8	㉞	10	㉟	3

Worksheet 40

①	6	②	10	③	6	④	6	⑤	6	⑥	10	⑦	9
⑧	5	⑨	3	⑩	7	⑪	3	⑫	4	⑬	10	⑭	8
⑮	7	⑯	10	⑰	3	⑱	6	⑲	6	⑳	3	㉑	7
㉒	5	㉓	5	㉔	8	㉕	7	㉖	8	㉗	7	㉘	3
㉙	7	㉚	7	㉛	4	㉜	4	㉝	7	㉞	10	㉟	10

Worksheet 41

①	8	②	7	③	6	④	10	⑤	10	⑥	9	⑦	9
⑧	3	⑨	3	⑩	4	⑪	5	⑫	4	⑬	7	⑭	4
⑮	4	⑯	9	⑰	10	⑱	2	⑲	3	⑳	9	㉑	7
㉒	7	㉓	10	㉔	10	㉕	6	㉖	3	㉗	2	㉘	6
㉙	7	㉚	3	㉛	8	㉜	8	㉝	4	㉞	10	㉟	6

Worksheet 42

①	8	②	7	③	2	④	3	⑤	10	⑥	2	⑦	6
⑧	8	⑨	8	⑩	9	⑪	10	⑫	10	⑬	9	⑭	2
⑮	6	⑯	5	⑰	5	⑱	2	⑲	8	⑳	7	㉑	2
㉒	10	㉓	9	㉔	2	㉕	3	㉖	9	㉗	10	㉘	3
㉙	6	㉚	8	㉛	8	㉜	8	㉝	3	㉞	7	㉟	5

Worksheet 43

①	10	②	2	③	10	④	3	⑤	6	⑥	2	⑦	5
⑧	10	⑨	7	⑩	10	⑪	7	⑫	8	⑬	5	⑭	7
⑮	9	⑯	5	⑰	9	⑱	9	⑲	4	⑳	10	㉑	10
㉒	9	㉓	5	㉔	8	㉕	2	㉖	7	㉗	8	㉘	8
㉙	5	㉚	2	㉛	4	㉜	2	㉝	10	㉞	8	㉟	3

Worksheet 44

①	10	②	3	③	4	④	4	⑤	10	⑥	5	⑦	9
⑧	5	⑨	10	⑩	2	⑪	9	⑫	9	⑬	5	⑭	10
⑮	2	⑯	6	⑰	4	⑱	10	⑲	6	⑳	4	㉑	9
㉒	4	㉓	4	㉔	5	㉕	4	㉖	2	㉗	6	㉘	7
㉙	10	㉚	4	㉛	9	㉜	10	㉝	5	㉞	7	㉟	8

Worksheet 45

①	3	②	3	③	4	④	9	⑤	2	⑥	2	⑦	5
⑧	2	⑨	10	⑩	10	⑪	8	⑫	5	⑬	6	⑭	10
⑮	4	⑯	4	⑰	4	⑱	2	⑲	7	⑳	6	㉑	5
㉒	6	㉓	7	㉔	10	㉕	7	㉖	8	㉗	6	㉘	2
㉙	4	㉚	7	㉛	9	㉜	4	㉝	4	㉞	7	㉟	3

Worksheet 46

①	6	②	5	③	5	④	9	⑤	8	⑥	6	⑦	9
⑧	6	⑨	10	⑩	3	⑪	6	⑫	5	⑬	6	⑭	2
⑮	7	⑯	7	⑰	9	⑱	8	⑲	2	⑳	8	㉑	7
㉒	10	㉓	4	㉔	8	㉕	2	㉖	5	㉗	6	㉘	2
㉙	9	㉚	6	㉛	2	㉜	7	㉝	6	㉞	9	㉟	4

Worksheet 47

①	7	②	4	③	2	④	3	⑤	9	⑥	9	⑦	7
⑧	8	⑨	5	⑩	4	⑪	9	⑫	5	⑬	2	⑭	6
⑮	6	⑯	8	⑰	9	⑱	4	⑲	10	⑳	8	㉑	6
㉒	8	㉓	4	㉔	9	㉕	8	㉖	8	㉗	5	㉘	9
㉙	7	㉚	2	㉛	5	㉜	8	㉝	10	㉞	8	㉟	3

Worksheet 48

①	7	②	7	③	7	④	4	⑤	10	⑥	5	⑦	3
⑧	10	⑨	4	⑩	5	⑪	9	⑫	2	⑬	6	⑭	8
⑮	5	⑯	10	⑰	5	⑱	3	⑲	7	⑳	3	㉑	4
㉒	4	㉓	10	㉔	8	㉕	3	㉖	5	㉗	3	㉘	8
㉙	4	㉚	10	㉛	2	㉜	10	㉝	8	㉞	3	㉟	7

Worksheet 49

①	5	②	2	③	9	④	5	⑤	2	⑥	6	⑦	4
⑧	6	⑨	4	⑩	9	⑪	8	⑫	9	⑬	8	⑭	9
⑮	9	⑯	10	⑰	2	⑱	5	⑲	6	⑳	8	㉑	10
㉒	7	㉓	7	㉔	4	㉕	9	㉖	10	㉗	3	㉘	5
㉙	2	㉚	9	㉛	8	㉜	8	㉝	5	㉞	9	㉟	4

Worksheet 50

① 8	② 6	③ 10	④ 3	⑤ 7	⑥ 3	⑦ 2
⑧ 5	⑨ 8	⑩ 10	⑪ 8	⑫ 4	⑬ 7	⑭ 10
⑮ 9	⑯ 4	⑰ 8	⑱ 2	⑲ 3	⑳ 7	㉑ 6
㉒ 8	㉓ 9	㉔ 4	㉕ 7	㉖ 8	㉗ 8	㉘ 8
㉙ 8	㉚ 7	㉛ 2	㉜ 8	㉝ 9	㉞ 2	㉟ 6

Worksheet 51

① 4	② 10	③ 10	④ 3	⑤ 11	⑥ 12	⑦ 7
⑧ 12	⑨ 2	⑩ 12	⑪ 10	⑫ 11	⑬ 0	⑭ 11
⑮ 6	⑯ 11	⑰ 0	⑱ 3	⑲ 8	⑳ 0	㉑ 1
㉒ 8	㉓ 9	㉔ 10	㉕ 10	㉖ 7	㉗ 3	㉘ 4
㉙ 3	㉚ 12	㉛ 8	㉜ 11	㉝ 3	㉞ 2	㉟ 6

Worksheet 52

① 6	② 5	③ 9	④ 2	⑤ 9	⑥ 8	⑦ 12
⑧ 10	⑨ 3	⑩ 9	⑪ 4	⑫ 2	⑬ 12	⑭ 11
⑮ 8	⑯ 0	⑰ 5	⑱ 4	⑲ 5	⑳ 8	㉑ 10
㉒ 6	㉓ 0	㉔ 12	㉕ 11	㉖ 2	㉗ 12	㉘ 3
㉙ 2	㉚ 0	㉛ 10	㉜ 10	㉝ 4	㉞ 0	㉟ 8

Worksheet 53

① 2	② 2	③ 6	④ 4	⑤ 4	⑥ 1	⑦ 5
⑧ 12	⑨ 8	⑩ 6	⑪ 7	⑫ 4	⑬ 8	⑭ 2
⑮ 8	⑯ 7	⑰ 3	⑱ 3	⑲ 2	⑳ 9	㉑ 10
㉒ 7	㉓ 11	㉔ 4	㉕ 8	㉖ 4	㉗ 4	㉘ 1
㉙ 12	㉚ 7	㉛ 1	㉜ 12	㉝ 3	㉞ 12	㉟ 1

Worksheet 54

① 9	② 12	③ 0	④ 1	⑤ 8	⑥ 9	⑦ 9
⑧ 1	⑨ 3	⑩ 8	⑪ 4	⑫ 1	⑬ 11	⑭ 10
⑮ 2	⑯ 3	⑰ 6	⑱ 5	⑲ 11	⑳ 2	㉑ 10
㉒ 9	㉓ 3	㉔ 0	㉕ 3	㉖ 1	㉗ 11	㉘ 3
㉙ 2	㉚ 12	㉛ 12	㉜ 9	㉝ 2	㉞ 2	㉟ 7

Worksheet 55

①	9	②	6	③	4	④	9	⑤	7	⑥	4	⑦	12
⑧	6	⑨	7	⑩	4	⑪	4	⑫	5	⑬	5	⑭	6
⑮	6	⑯	7	⑰	8	⑱	8	⑲	11	⑳	7	㉑	2
㉒	11	㉓	12	㉔	2	㉕	4	㉖	4	㉗	10	㉘	6
㉙	11	㉚	6	㉛	2	㉜	9	㉝	8	㉞	0	㉟	6

Worksheet 56

①	10	②	10	③	0	④	12	⑤	7	⑥	2	⑦	5
⑧	12	⑨	6	⑩	7	⑪	1	⑫	7	⑬	3	⑭	8
⑮	10	⑯	2	⑰	6	⑱	8	⑲	1	⑳	11	㉑	12
㉒	10	㉓	11	㉔	0	㉕	1	㉖	8	㉗	3	㉘	8
㉙	1	㉚	0	㉛	9	㉜	7	㉝	5	㉞	1	㉟	4

Worksheet 57

①	12	②	2	③	7	④	3	⑤	11	⑥	3	⑦	6
⑧	0	⑨	0	⑩	6	⑪	11	⑫	1	⑬	9	⑭	2
⑮	0	⑯	5	⑰	6	⑱	6	⑲	4	⑳	3	㉑	1
㉒	7	㉓	3	㉔	1	㉕	2	㉖	2	㉗	11	㉘	0
㉙	6	㉚	8	㉛	8	㉜	7	㉝	2	㉞	4	㉟	2

Worksheet 58

①	3	②	5	③	0	④	7	⑤	0	⑥	4	⑦	6
⑧	9	⑨	5	⑩	9	⑪	0	⑫	12	⑬	4	⑭	5
⑮	9	⑯	5	⑰	5	⑱	6	⑲	12	⑳	7	㉑	2
㉒	6	㉓	11	㉔	7	㉕	7	㉖	4	㉗	11	㉘	0
㉙	4	㉚	12	㉛	10	㉜	10	㉝	6	㉞	7	㉟	12

Worksheet 59

①	0	②	1	③	6	④	11	⑤	5	⑥	11	⑦	9
⑧	4	⑨	9	⑩	12	⑪	11	⑫	7	⑬	7	⑭	9
⑮	0	⑯	8	⑰	1	⑱	6	⑲	6	⑳	4	㉑	5
㉒	2	㉓	7	㉔	7	㉕	3	㉖	0	㉗	10	㉘	7
㉙	5	㉚	3	㉛	6	㉜	5	㉝	7	㉞	2	㉟	3

Worksheet 60

①	8	②	6	③	7	④	5	⑤	10	⑥	3	⑦	10
⑧	0	⑨	0	⑩	8	⑪	3	⑫	5	⑬	12	⑭	1
⑮	2	⑯	9	⑰	12	⑱	4	⑲	1	⑳	10	㉑	11
㉒	10	㉓	2	㉔	7	㉕	3	㉖	12	㉗	5	㉘	4
㉙	9	㉚	0	㉛	5	㉜	7	㉝	2	㉞	9	㉟	8

Worksheet 61

①	1	②	7	③	11	④	12	⑤	0	⑥	9	⑦	8
⑧	12	⑨	9	⑩	11	⑪	3	⑫	9	⑬	8	⑭	5
⑮	6	⑯	10	⑰	5	⑱	1	⑲	9	⑳	3	㉑	2
㉒	2	㉓	11	㉔	1	㉕	4	㉖	4	㉗	9	㉘	0
㉙	5	㉚	4	㉛	10	㉜	4	㉝	5	㉞	11	㉟	8

Worksheet 62

①	12	②	7	③	7	④	10	⑤	3	⑥	5	⑦	5
⑧	9	⑨	2	⑩	7	⑪	1	⑫	12	⑬	0	⑭	10
⑮	7	⑯	9	⑰	7	⑱	8	⑲	3	⑳	2	㉑	4
㉒	9	㉓	0	㉔	6	㉕	2	㉖	9	㉗	6	㉘	4
㉙	4	㉚	12	㉛	6	㉜	6	㉝	7	㉞	0	㉟	5

Worksheet 63

①	9	②	3	③	7	④	1	⑤	2	⑥	8	⑦	2
⑧	0	⑨	4	⑩	12	⑪	6	⑫	9	⑬	9	⑭	7
⑮	5	⑯	10	⑰	3	⑱	8	⑲	6	⑳	0	㉑	8
㉒	7	㉓	11	㉔	5	㉕	1	㉖	7	㉗	0	㉘	11
㉙	5	㉚	11	㉛	6	㉜	8	㉝	7	㉞	5	㉟	10

Worksheet 64

①	12	②	0	③	11	④	3	⑤	3	⑥	5	⑦	8
⑧	10	⑨	1	⑩	9	⑪	11	⑫	5	⑬	7	⑭	3
⑮	5	⑯	1	⑰	8	⑱	11	⑲	9	⑳	7	㉑	2
㉒	10	㉓	0	㉔	9	㉕	7	㉖	3	㉗	0	㉘	12
㉙	5	㉚	5	㉛	1	㉜	12	㉝	9	㉞	5	㉟	4

Worksheet 65

① 9	② 3	③ 9	④ 1	⑤ 6	⑥ 7	⑦ 1
⑧ 1	⑨ 10	⑩ 1	⑪ 3	⑫ 4	⑬ 9	⑭ 0
⑮ 2	⑯ 6	⑰ 8	⑱ 0	⑲ 8	⑳ 6	㉑ 10
㉒ 1	㉓ 11	㉔ 8	㉕ 10	㉖ 9	㉗ 3	㉘ 0
㉙ 11	㉚ 7	㉛ 3	㉜ 8	㉝ 5	㉞ 10	㉟ 1

Worksheet 66

① 2	② 5	③ 3	④ 10	⑤ 5	⑥ 0	⑦ 9
⑧ 0	⑨ 4	⑩ 12	⑪ 9	⑫ 12	⑬ 11	⑭ 2
⑮ 2	⑯ 7	⑰ 0	⑱ 10	⑲ 0	⑳ 2	㉑ 11
㉒ 1	㉓ 3	㉔ 0	㉕ 12	㉖ 2	㉗ 0	㉘ 5
㉙ 2	㉚ 6	㉛ 0	㉜ 12	㉝ 4	㉞ 12	㉟ 5

Worksheet 67

① 2	② 6	③ 10	④ 5	⑤ 3	⑥ 8	⑦ 4
⑧ 2	⑨ 12	⑩ 6	⑪ 1	⑫ 5	⑬ 12	⑭ 1
⑮ 1	⑯ 7	⑰ 7	⑱ 1	⑲ 4	⑳ 10	㉑ 9
㉒ 3	㉓ 12	㉔ 6	㉕ 2	㉖ 7	㉗ 3	㉘ 12
㉙ 1	㉚ 1	㉛ 2	㉜ 12	㉝ 2	㉞ 2	㉟ 2

Worksheet 68

① 12	② 11	③ 1	④ 7	⑤ 7	⑥ 3	⑦ 11
⑧ 9	⑨ 1	⑩ 7	⑪ 12	⑫ 3	⑬ 2	⑭ 8
⑮ 4	⑯ 11	⑰ 12	⑱ 1	⑲ 9	⑳ 2	㉑ 8
㉒ 11	㉓ 9	㉔ 6	㉕ 7	㉖ 8	㉗ 10	㉘ 10
㉙ 3	㉚ 8	㉛ 8	㉜ 0	㉝ 4	㉞ 10	㉟ 7

Worksheet 69

① 2	② 1	③ 8	④ 6	⑤ 1	⑥ 8	⑦ 8
⑧ 0	⑨ 6	⑩ 12	⑪ 12	⑫ 12	⑬ 0	⑭ 7
⑮ 8	⑯ 10	⑰ 9	⑱ 7	⑲ 1	⑳ 12	㉑ 4
㉒ 11	㉓ 11	㉔ 3	㉕ 8	㉖ 9	㉗ 12	㉘ 3
㉙ 9	㉚ 0	㉛ 11	㉜ 2	㉝ 4	㉞ 11	㉟ 6

Worksheet 70

①	4	②	2	③	9	④	0	⑤	2	⑥	1	⑦	0
⑧	7	⑨	10	⑩	6	⑪	5	⑫	5	⑬	6	⑭	2
⑮	1	⑯	8	⑰	8	⑱	0	⑲	7	⑳	5	㉑	10
㉒	3	㉓	5	㉔	6	㉕	9	㉖	12	㉗	12	㉘	5
㉙	0	㉚	11	㉛	0	㉜	2	㉝	3	㉞	5	㉟	0

Worksheet 71

①	10	②	6	③	10	④	12	⑤	9	⑥	7	⑦	3
⑧	7	⑨	9	⑩	4	⑪	7	⑫	8	⑬	7	⑭	7
⑮	10	⑯	6	⑰	3	⑱	9	⑲	5	⑳	10	㉑	8
㉒	4	㉓	12	㉔	10	㉕	9	㉖	6	㉗	2	㉘	10
㉙	12	㉚	8	㉛	9	㉜	9	㉝	6	㉞	4	㉟	2

Worksheet 72

①	4	②	3	③	5	④	6	⑤	11	⑥	3	⑦	12
⑧	10	⑨	2	⑩	8	⑪	7	⑫	10	⑬	3	⑭	11
⑮	4	⑯	6	⑰	4	⑱	11	⑲	2	⑳	11	㉑	9
㉒	9	㉓	9	㉔	5	㉕	9	㉖	6	㉗	7	㉘	9
㉙	5	㉚	9	㉛	8	㉜	2	㉝	7	㉞	8	㉟	4

Worksheet 73

①	8	②	11	③	11	④	11	⑤	4	⑥	4	⑦	3
⑧	9	⑨	6	⑩	3	⑪	5	⑫	2	⑬	9	⑭	12
⑮	3	⑯	3	⑰	11	⑱	8	⑲	10	⑳	7	㉑	5
㉒	10	㉓	12	㉔	6	㉕	9	㉖	10	㉗	12	㉘	2
㉙	5	㉚	7	㉛	9	㉜	4	㉝	9	㉞	4	㉟	8

Worksheet 74

①	10	②	6	③	12	④	6	⑤	12	⑥	2	⑦	9
⑧	8	⑨	5	⑩	4	⑪	3	⑫	8	⑬	7	⑭	6
⑮	9	⑯	2	⑰	12	⑱	6	⑲	4	⑳	9	㉑	9
㉒	6	㉓	2	㉔	8	㉕	6	㉖	11	㉗	2	㉘	2
㉙	9	㉚	8	㉛	2	㉜	12	㉝	9	㉞	2	㉟	12

Worksheet 75

① 8	② 8	③ 12	④ 8	⑤ 7	⑥ 10	⑦ 9
⑧ 12	⑨ 7	⑩ 6	⑪ 12	⑫ 6	⑬ 7	⑭ 3
⑮ 10	⑯ 2	⑰ 3	⑱ 7	⑲ 9	⑳ 8	㉑ 5
㉒ 4	㉓ 5	㉔ 11	㉕ 7	㉖ 9	㉗ 2	㉘ 6
㉙ 10	㉚ 9	㉛ 10	㉜ 9	㉝ 5	㉞ 7	㉟ 2

Worksheet 76

① 12	② 9	③ 12	④ 12	⑤ 9	⑥ 3	⑦ 4
⑧ 8	⑨ 4	⑩ 8	⑪ 9	⑫ 2	⑬ 11	⑭ 10
⑮ 12	⑯ 10	⑰ 12	⑱ 11	⑲ 4	⑳ 7	㉑ 6
㉒ 3	㉓ 11	㉔ 5	㉕ 3	㉖ 2	㉗ 5	㉘ 10
㉙ 12	㉚ 12	㉛ 4	㉜ 10	㉝ 10	㉞ 8	㉟ 3

Worksheet 77

① 9	② 6	③ 3	④ 6	⑤ 8	⑥ 3	⑦ 5
⑧ 5	⑨ 5	⑩ 8	⑪ 7	⑫ 3	⑬ 4	⑭ 5
⑮ 5	⑯ 6	⑰ 9	⑱ 12	⑲ 7	⑳ 10	㉑ 8
㉒ 11	㉓ 5	㉔ 3	㉕ 2	㉖ 2	㉗ 7	㉘ 6
㉙ 10	㉚ 8	㉛ 3	㉜ 3	㉝ 10	㉞ 4	㉟ 4

Worksheet 78

① 8	② 9	③ 11	④ 9	⑤ 12	⑥ 2	⑦ 8
⑧ 10	⑨ 10	⑩ 8	⑪ 4	⑫ 5	⑬ 7	⑭ 12
⑮ 7	⑯ 8	⑰ 12	⑱ 4	⑲ 2	⑳ 4	㉑ 3
㉒ 11	㉓ 6	㉔ 11	㉕ 8	㉖ 6	㉗ 9	㉘ 12
㉙ 4	㉚ 6	㉛ 11	㉜ 6	㉝ 4	㉞ 8	㉟ 11

Worksheet 79

① 2	② 7	③ 2	④ 4	⑤ 8	⑥ 5	⑦ 2
⑧ 12	⑨ 3	⑩ 2	⑪ 4	⑫ 6	⑬ 11	⑭ 11
⑮ 12	⑯ 10	⑰ 7	⑱ 7	⑲ 11	⑳ 4	㉑ 4
㉒ 6	㉓ 12	㉔ 4	㉕ 8	㉖ 9	㉗ 12	㉘ 11
㉙ 7	㉚ 7	㉛ 10	㉜ 6	㉝ 7	㉞ 9	㉟ 11

Worksheet 80

①	4	②	7	③	7	④	6	⑤	8	⑥	10	⑦	11
⑧	2	⑨	5	⑩	12	⑪	10	⑫	11	⑬	9	⑭	11
⑮	11	⑯	9	⑰	12	⑱	11	⑲	10	⑳	4	㉑	11
㉒	11	㉓	6	㉔	11	㉕	10	㉖	5	㉗	4	㉘	11
㉙	6	㉚	2	㉛	9	㉜	7	㉝	9	㉞	3	㉟	4

Worksheet 81

①	5	②	8	③	9	④	3	⑤	12	⑥	4	⑦	8
⑧	4	⑨	3	⑩	7	⑪	4	⑫	3	⑬	3	⑭	5
⑮	6	⑯	8	⑰	8	⑱	6	⑲	6	⑳	6	㉑	9
㉒	2	㉓	6	㉔	6	㉕	5	㉖	2	㉗	10	㉘	11
㉙	11	㉚	2	㉛	7	㉜	9	㉝	9	㉞	6	㉟	9

Worksheet 82

①	2	②	9	③	11	④	5	⑤	6	⑥	11	⑦	4
⑧	5	⑨	4	⑩	4	⑪	11	⑫	3	⑬	8	⑭	7
⑮	7	⑯	3	⑰	8	⑱	9	⑲	3	⑳	7	㉑	10
㉒	2	㉓	6	㉔	4	㉕	12	㉖	11	㉗	10	㉘	12
㉙	8	㉚	12	㉛	4	㉜	12	㉝	7	㉞	4	㉟	3

Worksheet 83

①	3	②	11	③	12	④	8	⑤	8	⑥	12	⑦	12
⑧	4	⑨	4	⑩	4	⑪	9	⑫	3	⑬	5	⑭	3
⑮	5	⑯	8	⑰	4	⑱	3	⑲	8	⑳	4	㉑	7
㉒	2	㉓	4	㉔	8	㉕	8	㉖	2	㉗	11	㉘	7
㉙	11	㉚	7	㉛	3	㉜	12	㉝	4	㉞	7	㉟	9

Worksheet 84

①	7	②	5	③	10	④	6	⑤	10	⑥	4	⑦	8
⑧	6	⑨	6	⑩	3	⑪	12	⑫	10	⑬	2	⑭	12
⑮	4	⑯	6	⑰	4	⑱	8	⑲	2	⑳	4	㉑	4
㉒	5	㉓	3	㉔	11	㉕	5	㉖	3	㉗	6	㉘	10
㉙	5	㉚	10	㉛	3	㉜	6	㉝	5	㉞	8	㉟	4

Worksheet 85

①	2	②	8	③	3	④	11	⑤	10	⑥	9	⑦	6
⑧	9	⑨	9	⑩	12	⑪	6	⑫	7	⑬	10	⑭	3
⑮	11	⑯	3	⑰	10	⑱	4	⑲	5	⑳	5	㉑	5
㉒	12	㉓	12	㉔	4	㉕	7	㉖	8	㉗	3	㉘	8
㉙	9	㉚	4	㉛	11	㉜	2	㉝	9	㉞	3	㉟	12

Worksheet 86

①	6	②	6	③	5	④	2	⑤	2	⑥	2	⑦	9
⑧	2	⑨	3	⑩	5	⑪	8	⑫	11	⑬	11	⑭	12
⑮	8	⑯	7	⑰	10	⑱	12	⑲	4	⑳	9	㉑	8
㉒	5	㉓	7	㉔	3	㉕	6	㉖	3	㉗	12	㉘	4
㉙	12	㉚	11	㉛	8	㉜	10	㉝	3	㉞	5	㉟	6

Worksheet 87

①	9	②	9	③	2	④	6	⑤	10	⑥	4	⑦	2
⑧	5	⑨	12	⑩	7	⑪	5	⑫	8	⑬	5	⑭	8
⑮	3	⑯	4	⑰	6	⑱	8	⑲	9	⑳	12	㉑	9
㉒	3	㉓	7	㉔	6	㉕	6	㉖	9	㉗	7	㉘	10
㉙	8	㉚	10	㉛	6	㉜	5	㉝	4	㉞	7	㉟	4

Worksheet 88

①	7	②	11	③	5	④	7	⑤	8	⑥	3	⑦	10
⑧	10	⑨	9	⑩	10	⑪	8	⑫	12	⑬	2	⑭	2
⑮	3	⑯	6	⑰	8	⑱	10	⑲	7	⑳	8	㉑	2
㉒	8	㉓	2	㉔	2	㉕	2	㉖	4	㉗	7	㉘	11
㉙	8	㉚	10	㉛	9	㉜	11	㉝	9	㉞	6	㉟	4

Worksheet 89

①	3	②	4	③	7	④	3	⑤	5	⑥	3	⑦	4
⑧	3	⑨	11	⑩	10	⑪	7	⑫	2	⑬	9	⑭	10
⑮	8	⑯	2	⑰	9	⑱	5	⑲	3	⑳	9	㉑	8
㉒	9	㉓	4	㉔	8	㉕	11	㉖	7	㉗	6	㉘	5
㉙	9	㉚	11	㉛	12	㉜	12	㉝	9	㉞	12	㉟	8

Worksheet 90

①	5	②	4	③	12	④	5	⑤	5	⑥	7	⑦	7
⑧	5	⑨	12	⑩	11	⑪	5	⑫	10	⑬	11	⑭	10
⑮	4	⑯	10	⑰	8	⑱	8	⑲	12	⑳	3	㉑	9
㉒	8	㉓	2	㉔	10	㉕	2	㉖	11	㉗	7	㉘	12
㉙	10	㉚	4	㉛	5	㉜	2	㉝	5	㉞	4	㉟	6

Worksheet 91

①	3	②	3	③	10	④	7	⑤	12	⑥	2	⑦	4
⑧	12	⑨	11	⑩	7	⑪	3	⑫	11	⑬	9	⑭	4
⑮	2	⑯	4	⑰	7	⑱	2	⑲	7	⑳	4	㉑	8
㉒	10	㉓	6	㉔	12	㉕	5	㉖	8	㉗	3	㉘	4
㉙	12	㉚	7	㉛	11	㉜	2	㉝	5	㉞	12	㉟	9

Worksheet 92

①	10	②	11	③	7	④	2	⑤	10	⑥	6	⑦	7
⑧	9	⑨	9	⑩	7	⑪	8	⑫	4	⑬	12	⑭	7
⑮	3	⑯	10	⑰	3	⑱	12	⑲	6	⑳	6	㉑	5
㉒	10	㉓	12	㉔	5	㉕	10	㉖	8	㉗	10	㉘	6
㉙	2	㉚	3	㉛	8	㉜	8	㉝	6	㉞	7	㉟	9

Worksheet 93

①	3	②	10	③	2	④	4	⑤	10	⑥	10	⑦	9
⑧	3	⑨	3	⑩	9	⑪	8	⑫	9	⑬	4	⑭	4
⑮	6	⑯	3	⑰	7	⑱	2	⑲	7	⑳	2	㉑	5
㉒	7	㉓	7	㉔	11	㉕	8	㉖	12	㉗	6	㉘	8
㉙	3	㉚	3	㉛	11	㉜	7	㉝	2	㉞	5	㉟	7

Worksheet 94

①	7	②	5	③	3	④	9	⑤	6	⑥	5	⑦	6
⑧	6	⑨	6	⑩	2	⑪	9	⑫	8	⑬	7	⑭	8
⑮	10	⑯	10	⑰	10	⑱	4	⑲	6	⑳	2	㉑	10
㉒	5	㉓	4	㉔	9	㉕	9	㉖	9	㉗	6	㉘	8
㉙	5	㉚	3	㉛	3	㉜	3	㉝	9	㉞	7	㉟	2

Worksheet 95

① 9	② 3	③ 9	④ 9	⑤ 12	⑥ 8	⑦ 3
⑧ 2	⑨ 8	⑩ 3	⑪ 2	⑫ 2	⑬ 3	⑭ 6
⑮ 3	⑯ 9	⑰ 7	⑱ 2	⑲ 8	⑳ 9	㉑ 7
㉒ 3	㉓ 10	㉔ 12	㉕ 5	㉖ 3	㉗ 6	㉘ 3
㉙ 11	㉚ 8	㉛ 5	㉜ 2	㉝ 9	㉞ 10	㉟ 11

Worksheet 96

① 9	② 10	③ 12	④ 2	⑤ 6	⑥ 3	⑦ 8
⑧ 4	⑨ 10	⑩ 5	⑪ 7	⑫ 5	⑬ 7	⑭ 7
⑮ 12	⑯ 11	⑰ 10	⑱ 4	⑲ 12	⑳ 4	㉑ 5
㉒ 8	㉓ 8	㉔ 5	㉕ 10	㉖ 8	㉗ 2	㉘ 6
㉙ 7	㉚ 9	㉛ 11	㉜ 12	㉝ 12	㉞ 9	㉟ 8

Worksheet 97

① 12	② 11	③ 2	④ 2	⑤ 6	⑥ 3	⑦ 8
⑧ 11	⑨ 5	⑩ 11	⑪ 3	⑫ 6	⑬ 10	⑭ 12
⑮ 4	⑯ 2	⑰ 5	⑱ 12	⑲ 3	⑳ 10	㉑ 2
㉒ 6	㉓ 10	㉔ 9	㉕ 9	㉖ 7	㉗ 3	㉘ 9
㉙ 6	㉚ 6	㉛ 2	㉜ 11	㉝ 5	㉞ 12	㉟ 3

Worksheet 98

① 3	② 8	③ 2	④ 8	⑤ 2	⑥ 10	⑦ 12
⑧ 4	⑨ 8	⑩ 5	⑪ 2	⑫ 9	⑬ 4	⑭ 11
⑮ 5	⑯ 5	⑰ 5	⑱ 7	⑲ 11	⑳ 4	㉑ 11
㉒ 3	㉓ 7	㉔ 7	㉕ 8	㉖ 5	㉗ 12	㉘ 3
㉙ 10	㉚ 4	㉛ 7	㉜ 2	㉝ 12	㉞ 2	㉟ 6

Worksheet 99

① 3	② 7	③ 4	④ 6	⑤ 4	⑥ 8	⑦ 6
⑧ 3	⑨ 6	⑩ 12	⑪ 4	⑫ 11	⑬ 6	⑭ 4
⑮ 9	⑯ 10	⑰ 9	⑱ 5	⑲ 4	⑳ 10	㉑ 9
㉒ 2	㉓ 4	㉔ 6	㉕ 9	㉖ 5	㉗ 12	㉘ 7
㉙ 9	㉚ 2	㉛ 9	㉜ 11	㉝ 5	㉞ 2	㉟ 8

Worksheet   100

①	2	②	2	③	10	④	11	⑤	7	⑥	7	⑦	6
⑧	7	⑨	6	⑩	12	⑪	10	⑫	5	⑬	6	⑭	11
⑮	7	⑯	6	⑰	5	⑱	3	⑲	4	⑳	5	㉑	2
㉒	8	㉓	9	㉔	5	㉕	9	㉖	5	㉗	7	㉘	10
㉙	9	㉚	9	㉛	8	㉜	12	㉝	9	㉞	7	㉟	12

Did You Like This Book?

I searched online to find basic math worksheets like these, but wasn't satisfied with what I found. I made these math worksheets for my children and students. Then I put them together in this workbook so that they would be available to other parents and teachers. Some of my objectives in making this workbook were:

- Including the answers at the back so parents or teachers could easily check the solutions.
- Numbering the exercises to make it easy to check the answers, and to allow teachers to assign groups of problems by number.
- Providing enough space for students to write their answers.
- Organizing the problems in a visually appealing way, and arranging the content so that the level of difficulty grows as the book progresses.
- Having designated room for students to write their name, and for parents or teachers to record the score and time.
- Making the book affordable. I hope that you believe this workbook to be a good value.

I hope that you found this workbook to be useful. I would be very appreciative of any feedback that you may choose to leave at www.amazon.com. This would also be very helpful for any other parents or teachers who are searching for math workbooks.

Thank You,
Anne Fairbanks

Made in the USA
San Bernardino, CA
31 July 2014